Transcendental Style in Film: Ozu, Bresson, Dreyer

Transcendental Style in Film: Ozu, Bresson, Dreyer

Paul Schrader

DA CAPO PRESS

Library of Congress Cataloging in Publication Data

Schrader, Paul, 1946-
  Transcendental style in film: Ozu, Bresson, Dreyer / Paul
Schrader.
    (A Da Capo paperback)
    Reprint. Originally published: Berkeley: University of California
Press, c1972.
    Bibliography: p.
    Includes index.
    1. Motion pictures—Aesthetics. 2. Ozu, Yasujirō, 1903-1963—
Criticism and interpretation. 3. Bresson, Robert—Criticism and
interpretation. 4. Dreyer, Carl Theodor, 1889-1968—Criticism and
interpretation. I. Title.
PN1995.S417   1988
791.43'01—dc19   88-15974
ISBN 0-306-80335-6 (pbk.)

This Da Capo Press paperback edition of *Transcendental Style in Film* is an
unabridged republication of the edition published in Berkeley in 1972. It is
reprinted by arrangement with the University of California Press.

Published by Da Capo Press, Inc.
A Member of the Perseus Books Group
Visit us on the World Wide Web at www.dacapopress.com

Printed and bound in Great Britain by
Marston Lindsay Ross International Ltd,
Oxfordshire

Religion and art
are parallel lines
which intersect only at infinity,
and meet in God.

GERARDUS VAN DER LEEUW

Acknowledgments

I am grateful to Jim Kitses, Nicholas Wolterstorff, Donald Richie, Rudolf Arnheim, Donald Skoller, Stephen Mamber, James Blue and my publisher, Ernest Callenbach, for reading the manuscript in whole or part and offering advice, support, and suggestions. Also thanks to the American Film Institute for screening films at my request and assisting in several translations, and to Shochiku Co., Ltd., for stills.

This book is dedicated to my father, without whom it would not have been written.

Introduction

In recent years film has developed a transcendental style, a style which has been used by various artists in diverse cultures to express the Holy. Just as anthropologists at the turn of the century discovered that artisans in unrelated cultures had found similar ways to express similar spiritual emotions, so, in cinema, unrelated film-makers have created a consensus of transcendental style. The style is not intrinsically transcendental or religious, but it represents a way (a *tao*, in the broadest sense of the term) to approach the Transcendent. The matter being transcended is different in each case, but the goal and the method are, at their purest, the same.

Yasujiro Ozu in Japan, Robert Bresson in France, to a lesser degree Carl Dreyer in Denmark, and other directors in various countries have forged a remarkably common film form. This common form was not determined by the film-makers' personalities, culture, politics, economics, or morality. It is instead the result of two universal contingencies: the desire to express the Transcendent in art and the nature of the film medium. In the final result no other factors can give this style its universality.

The "spiritual universality" of transcendental style may be variously interpreted by theologians, aestheticians, and psychologists; but it can only be demonstrated by critics. At this point everyone must return to the evidence; one must analyze the films, scenes, and frames, hoping to extract the universal from the particular.

Because transcendental style is fundamentally just that, a style, it can be isolated, analyzed, and defined. Although transcendental style, like any form of transcendental art, strives toward the ineffable and invisible, it is neither ineffable nor invisible itself. Transcendental style uses precise temporal means —camera angles, dialogue, editing—for predetermined

Christ Pantocrator, *c.* 1100, dome mosaic at Daphni.

transcendental ends. It has three distinct stages and those stages can be studied both individually and as part of the larger whole.

Transcendental style is not a vague label like "religious film" which can be attached to films which feature certain religious themes and evoke the appropriate emotions; it is not a catchbasin for all the sniffles, sobs and goosebumps one has experienced at religious films. It is neither a personal vision nor an official catechism. It is not necessarily typified by Joan at the stake, Christ on the Mount, or St. Francis among the flowers; it is not necessarily suffering, preaching, or good will among men. It is only *necessarily* a style.

If a critic hopes to extract this style and its component parts from the individual artists who employ it, from the cultures which influence those artists, and from the emotions it must use and transform, he must have some fairly precise critical tools (and even then it's like trying to separate sound from the waves it travels on). A term like "transcendental," after all, is almost nonfunctional in art criticism, and "style" is little better. Causing more problems than it solves "transcendental" has fallen under the jurisdiction of journalese, particularly among film critics. "Transcendental" is currently a catchall term for the imprecise critic: a film's plot, setting, acting, theme, and direction are all spoken of as transcending each other or themselves, and "style" can refer to anything from a camera angle to a way of life.

"Transcendental style," however, can be a useful term in film criticism, and when analyzing the films of certain film-makers, such as Ozu, Bresson, and Dreyer, it can be indispensable. The understandable reluctance of aestheticians and serious film critics to employ the concept of transcendence has caused these films to be underestimated and misinterpreted to varying degrees, and evaluated within critical patterns for which they were not intended. But before these terms can be of any use to a critic they must have meaning: he must know what is "transcendental" and what is "style." And knowing this, he not only has a term which denotes a specific style, but also the critical method with which to analyze it.

Definition No. 1: Transcendental

The Transcendent is beyond normal sense experience, and that which it transcends is, by definition, the immanent. Beyond this truism there is little agreement about the nature of the transcendental in life and art. Transcendence has been a subject of the philosophical debate since Plato, of the aesthetic debate since Plotinus, and has been variously interpreted by philosophers, aestheticians, theologians, anthropologists, and psychologists. Part of the confusion is semantic; the term "transcendental" can have different meanings for different writers. It can mean, directly or indirectly: (1) the Transcendent, the Holy or Ideal itself, or what Rudolf Otto called the "Wholly Other," (2) the transcendental, human acts or artifacts which express something of the Transcendent, or what Mircea Eliade in his anthropological study of comparative religions calls "hierophanies," (3) transcendence, the human religious experience which may be motivated by either a deep psychological need or neurosis (Freud), or by an external, "Other" force (Jung).

Similarly, these terms can refer to general varieties of sacred art: (1) works which *inform* the viewer/reader/listener about the Transcendent, which by their very definition must come directly from the Transcendent itself since no man can know about the Holy; works such as untampered nature (common revelation) and "divinely-inspired" Scriptures (special revelation), although this category may be only theoretical since even many theologians regard the various Scriptures as only expressive of the Holy, (2) works which *express* the Transcendent in human reflection, man-made, man-organized, or man-selected works which are more expressive of the Wholly Other than of their individual creators, works such as the Byzantine ikons or Zen gardens, (3) works which relate the human experience of transcendence, which *express* not the Transcendent but the human who experiences the Transcendent, works such as expressionist paintings or any of the many psychological novels about religious conversion.

The terms "Transcendent," "transcendental," and "transcendence" represent a hierarchy of the spiritual from the Other-oriented to the human-oriented. Because the Transcendent rarely speaks out on such matters, there is bound to be some semantic confusion over these terms. Philosophers and artists are human, and humans have often yielded to the temptation to cross-interpret from one category to the next, to define the Transcendent by the human experience of transcendence.

Carl Jung was reacting against this tendency when he wrote, "Every statement about the transcendental ought to be avoided because it is invariably a laughable presumption on the part of the human mind, unconscious of its limitations. Therefore, when God or Tao is named as a stirring of, or a condition of, the soul, something has been said about the knowable only, but nothing about the unknowable. Of the latter, nothing can be determined."[1]

Human works, accordingly, cannot *inform* one about the Transcendent, they can only be *expressive* of the Transcendent. This essay will concentrate on transcendental art, art which expresses the Transcendent in the human mirror.

By conjoining the words "transcendental," generally a religious term, and "art" into one term, "transcendental art," one implies that he considers religion and art homogeneous. This, of course, sections him off from the considerable body of critics who consider the transcendental outside the province of art. Transcendence in art is often equated with transcendence in religion because they both draw from a common ground of transcendental experience. Transcendence is the imperious experience; art and religion are its twin manifestations, as Clive Bell wrote, "Art and Religion are the two roads by which men escape from circumstance to ecstasy. Art and Religion are means to similar states of mind."[2] Transcendental art is not sectarian, however: "Art can be religious," the late Gerardus van der Leeuw wrote, "or can appear to be religious; but it can be neither Mohammedan nor Buddhist nor Christian. There is no Christian art, any more than there is a Christian science. There is only art which has stood before the Holy."[3] The proper function of transcendental art is, therefore, to express the Holy itself (the Transcendent), and not to express or illustrate holy feelings.

CRITICISM AND TRANSCENDENTAL ART

The critical queasiness about transcendental art is understandable because the more pure and absolute such an art becomes the less useful it is. At its best transcendental art is a self-destructive process. In his study of traditional Christian and Oriental art (essentially transcendental art), Ananda Coomaraswamy writes, "Art, even the highest, is only a means to an end, even scriptural art is only a manner of 'seeing through a glass, darkly,' and although this is far better than not to see at all, the utility of iconography must come to an end when the vision is 'face to face.' "[4] Like transcendental religion, transcendental art merges with mysticism: "Absolute religion is mysticism; it is without shape and without sound. Absolute art can neither be seen nor heard."[5] A critical devotion to the transcendent in art may eventually lead to the end of creative production, as it did for Coleridge after 1815. Both religion and art are highly partisan, and when conjoined under the banner of transcendental expression they will abide no peers. Transcendental art may tolerate other forms of expression, but it cannot accept them as equal or alternative. Good criticism is eclectic, transcendental art is autocratic; they have made understandably poor bedfellows.

Like transcendental art, the criticism of transcendental art is a self-destructive process. It continually deals in contradictions—verbalizations of the ineffable. The concept of transcendental expression in religion or in art necessarily implies a contradiction. Transcendental expression in religion and art attempts to bring man as close to the ineffable, invisible and unknowable as words, images, and ideas can take him. Like the artist, the critic knows that his task is futile, and that his most eloquent statements can only lead to silence. The critical inquiry, Roger Fry stated, ends at the gulf of mysticism.[6]

Although a critic cannot analyze the Transcendent, he can describe the immanent and the manner in which it is transcended. He can discover how the immanent is expressive of the Transcendent.

DEFINITION No. 2: STYLE

Like "transcendence," the term "style" is susceptible to semantic confusion. It can have various meanings: it can mean, as Wylie Sypher states, "a contemporary view of the world"[7] expressed by a particular geographic-historical culture, or it can mean the individual expression Raymond Durgnat describes as the "creation of a personal, a subjective, a 'non-objective' world,"[8] or it can mean what Heinrich Wolfflin called a "general representative form."[9] The style described in this essay is a style in the way that Wolfflin used that term, a style like the primitive or classic styles, the expression of similar ideas in similar forms by divergent cultures. The first two of the above-mentioned uses of style, Sypher's and Durgnat's, respectively describe the cultural and personal qualities of a work of art, and therefore are most appropriate for art which expresses the human experience rather than the Transcendent itself. Wolfflin's use of style, on the other hand, is concerned with what is universal rather than particular in the various means of expression, and therefore is ideally suited to describe a style which seeks to express the Wholly Other through divergent cultures and personalities.

DEFINITION No. 3: TRANSCENDENTAL STYLE

Semantically, transcendental style is simply this: a general representative filmic form which expresses the Transcendent. As used in this essay, transcendental style refers to a specific filmic form, although there could conceivably be several transcendental styles in film. The critical approach I associate with the term "transcendental style" echoes the above definition and may be loosely called an Eliade-Wolfflin method.* This method is, again quite simply, a study of contemporary artistic hierophanies through the analysis of common film forms and techniques.

The critical method used in this essay is based on two premises: (1) that there are such things as hierophanies, expressions of the transcendent in society (Eliade); (2) that there are common representative artistic forms shared by divergent cultures (Wolfflin). Transcendental style is each of these.

Any film (or phenomenon), of course, can be discussed from any critical perspective. No definition of "transcendental" or "style" monopolizes the discussion of any work of art. Films employing transcendental style may be studied from the cultural or personal perspective, and they usually are. Although the critical method I associate with the term "transcendental style" does not have a monopoly over the discussion of the films of directors like Ozu and Bresson, I think it has a priority. In most films the film-maker's ability to express his culture or personality is more important than his inability to transcend them, but when a film does seem to have that genuinely transcendent, "Other" quality, such as Ozu's *Late Autumn* or Bresson's *Diary of a Country Priest*, the cultural and personal approaches, although perhaps factually accurate, are inadequate. A cultural or personal approach necessarily disregards the unique quality of transcendental style: its ability to transcend culture and personality. There is a spiritual truth that can be achieved by objectively setting objects and pictures side by side that cannot be obtained through a subjective personal or cultural approach to those objects.

The study of transcendental style reveals a "universal form of representation." That form is remarkably unified: the

---

* It will shortly become obvious, however, that my method does justice to neither Eliade nor Wolfflin. I am more interested in contemporary and self-conscious artistic techniques than Eliade, and more interested in metaphysical meaning than Wolfflin. The term Eliade-Wolfflin is more associative than descriptive.

common expression of the Transcendent in motion pictures. The differences among the films of Ozu, Bresson, and Dreyer are cultural and personal; their similarities are stylistic, and represent a unified reflection of the Transcendent on film.

Toward a Working Definition

Many film-makers have employed the transcendental style, but few have had the devotion, the rigor, and the outright fanaticism to employ it exclusively. Elements of the transcendental style can be detected in the films of many other directors: Antonioni, Rossellini, Pasolini, Boetticher, Renoir, Mizoguchi, Bunuel, Warhol, Michael Snow, and Bruce Baillie. One of the complications of discussing transcendental style is that it enters in and does business with all sorts of styles. Dreyer's *The Passion of Joan of Arc* may be described as a transcendental film which indulges in expressionism, Pasolini's *The Gospel According to St. Matthew* as a transcendental film which gives way to Marxist realism, and Boetticher's *Seven Men From Now* as a transcendental film which yields to psychological realism.

Two directors have defined the transcendental style— Yasujiro Ozu in the East and Robert Bresson in the West. They have taken an intellectual, formalistic approach to film, and their films are the culminant products of erudite and sophisticated cultures. The family-office cycle of Ozu's later films and the prison cycle of Bresson's middle films construct a similar style to express the Transcendent. Carl Dreyer employs the transcendental style extensively, although his films are not prescriptive of the style, as are Ozu's and Bresson's. Dreyer expressed the Transcendent in a manner similar to Bresson, notably in *Ordet*, but he never completed a cycle of films employing the transcendental style. This essay could be extended to consider additional examples of the partial (and partially successful) use of transcendental style in certain of the films of Budd Boetticher and Roberto Rossellini. Although these would be valuable variations on the theme, three examples should be sufficient to carry the weight of the argument.

Transcendental style seeks to maximize the mystery of existence; it eschews all conventional interpretations of reality: realism, naturalism, psychologism, romanticism, expressionism, impressionism, and, finally, rationalism. To the transcendental artist rationalism is only one of many approaches to life, not an imperative. "If everything is explained by understandable causal necessities," abbot Amédée Ayfre wrote, "or by objective determinism, even if their precise nature remains unknown, then nothing is sacred."[10] The enemy of transcendence is immanence, whether it is external (realism, rationalism) or internal (psychologism, expressionism). To the transcendental artist these conventional interpretations of reality are emotional and rational constructs devised by man to dilute or explain away the transcendental.

In motion pictures these constructs take the form of what Robert Bresson has called "screens,"[11] clues or study guides which help the viewer "understand" the event: plot, acting, characterization, camerawork, music, dialogue, editing. In films of transcendental style these elements are, in popular terms, "nonexpressive" (that is they are not expressive of culture or personality); they are reduced to stasis. Transcendental style *stylizes* reality by eliminating (or nearly eliminating) those elements which are primarily expressive of human experience, thereby robbing the conventional interpretations of reality of their relevance and power. Transcendental style, like the mass, transforms experience into a repeatable ritual which can be repeatedly transcended.

In this essay there will be many occasions to draw comparisons between transcendental style and earlier means of religious and artistic expression. The most irreducible of these metaphors is between transcendental style and primitive art primarily because primitive art has always been closely associated with primitive religious belief. If one divides art into primitivism and classicism as Waldermar Doenna has done,[12] transcendental style invariably falls into the primitivism column. Using Deonna's dichotomies, transcendental style chooses irrationalism over rationalism, repetition over variation, sacred over profane, the deific over the humanistic, intellectual realism over optical realism, two-dimensional vision over three-dimensional vision, tradition over experiment, anonymity over individualization. (The primitive-classical dichotomy is not necessarily a chronological one; they can be found in all cultures.) The reason for the affinity between transcendental style and primitivism is obvious: both have "a world view which encloses mankind and

the All in a deeply felt unity, which constitutes the essence of
their religiousness."[13] Whenever religious primitivism emerges
from a post-Hellenic culture, a new artistic style results, whether
it be Byzantine, Gothic, or suprematist. In cinema, the new form
is transcendental style.*

In each of the three chapters that follow there will be
appropriate references to earlier artistic-religious expression:
Ozu to the Zen arts of painting, gardening, and haiku; Bresson
to Byzantine iconography; Dreyer to Gothic architecture.

This essay hopes to posit the transcendental style and
explain some of its aesthetics. I have not attempted a full analysis
of the directors since I am primarily interested in these film-
makers to the extent that their films reveal the transcendental
style. From a study of Ozu's later family-office cycle of films one
can extricate the transcendental style from an indigenous
(Oriental) culture and examine how it functions both in and out
of its culture. In Bresson's prison cycle films, Western history

* In relation to transcendental style, the terms "primitive" and
"traditional" invite some inevitable semantic confusion. Although these
terms are open to various interpretations, for the purpose of this book I
will define my use of them. All three terms belong to the category of
transcendental art, art which is expressive of the transcendent. Primitive
art denotes transcendental art in a pre-Hellenic culture (and such cultures
can still exist). It is an art of superstition and magic: "all the indications
point to the fact that it was the instrument of a magical technique and as
such had a thoroughly pragmatic function aimed entirely at direct economic
objectives. This magic apparently had nothing in common with what we
understand by religion; it knew no prayers, revered no sacred powers,
and was connected with no other-worldly spiritual beings of any kind of
faith, and there failed to fulfill what has been described as the minimum
condition of an authentic religion" (Arnold Hauser, *The Social History of
Art* [New York: Vintage Books, 1951], I, p. 7). Traditional art denotes
transcendental art in a post-Hellenic culture. It is represented by a civilized
religion with its own theology and aesthetics. Traditional art has reacted
to Hellenism by turning Platonic idealism to sacred objects. In traditional
art one can speak, as Ananda Coomaraswamy has, of a Christian and
Oriental *philosophy* of art. The once-superstitious artists now "believe in
a twofold order of reality, the one visible, palpable, and subordinate to
the essential laws of motion; the other invisible, intangible, 'spiritual,'
forming a mystic sphere which encompasses the first" (Lucien Lévy-Bruhl,
How Natives Think (London, 1926), p. 86). Transcendental style denotes a
transcendental art in a post-Renaissance culture. This term has no general
usage in art history and I use it to identify attempts by recent artists to
restore the sacred qualities of art to a culture which has felt the humanizing
effect of Greece and the individualizing effect of the Renaissance.

Left: Madonna and child icon, Tikhvin Monastery; right: *Virgin and Child*, by Master Michiel, Netherlands, 1520.
"Transcendental style chooses intellectual realism over optical realism, two-dimensional vision over three-dimensional vision, the deific over the humanistic."

and thought have already alienated the transcendental style from its culture; his films provide an excellent opportunity to study in depth and suggest how it actually "works" on the viewer. Dreyer's films, although less successful on the transcendental level, illustrate how the style (or a part of it) functions in a hostile environment.

The Conclusion will discuss some of the problems raised by a theory of transcendental style in the cinema.

I. Ozu

Yasujiro Ozu

The films of Yasujiro Ozu exemplify the transcendental style in the East. In his films this style is natural, indigenous, and commercially successful, largely because of the Japanese culture itself. The concept of transcendental experience is so intrinsic to Japanese (and Oriental) culture, that Ozu was able both to develop the transcendental style and to stay within the popular conventions of Japanese art. Ozu, often described as the "most Japanese of all directors," gained respect as a genre director and critical and financial success—rewards which no director interested in transcendental style could expect to reap in the West.

Oriental art in general and Zen art in particular aspire to the Transcendent. Like primitive art, traditional Oriental art makes no distinctions between the sacred and the secular. The Orient forged a lasting culture out of what the Neoplatonists and Scholastics hypothesized and in rare cases realized: an anonymous art in which "all that is true, by whomsoever it has been said, has its origin in the Spirit."[1] In Zen, this is expressed by R. H. Blyth: "The poetical and the religious are identical states of mind . . . to the religious all things are poetical . . . to the poetical all things are religious."[2] For thirteen hundred years Zen has cultivated the transcendental experience, and the Transcendent has found expression not only in religion and the arts, but also in a wide variety of "commonplace" activities. This expression of the Transcendent was not the perquisite of an intellectual or clerical elite. It became an endemic part of the Oriental heritage mainly through the arts, and no distinction was made between the fine and the manual arts. Zen dislikes the "odor of abstraction" which comes from a term like "transcendence," D. T. Suzuki points out, because in fact Zen dislikes any appeal to words. Acknowledging this semantic obstacle, it is safe to say, as Suzuki does, that Zen operates within the "realm of transcendence."[3]

Thus Ozu did not need to revive the expression of the Transcendent in Japan, or inject it into the Oriental culture, but only to adapt it to film. Ozu represents traditional Japanese thought and art, and he brings the weight of Oriental tradition to the modern, anarchic film medium. Donald Richie has schematized Japanese film directors, placing Kurosawa on the far left (modern) and Ozu on the far right (traditional).[4] Ozu was markedly conservative in subject matter and method (he was among the last Japanese directors to utilize sound or color), and he strove to put the old tradition in the new format. In Japan "modern civilization is only one hundred years old and is a veneer over a civilization which has endured for two millennia";[5] in Ozu's films Zen art and thought is the civilization, film is the veneer.

Although the Japanese cultural tradition afforded Ozu some luxuries, his task was not as easy as it may seem. Cinema has been one of the primary Westernizing influences in contemporary Japan, and in his striving for traditional values Ozu often ran contrary to current trends and is still regarded as reactionary by many Japanese youths. In a sense Ozu bucked fashion in his pursuit of a filmic transcendental style, but the resistance he met was relatively minor compared to the resistance encountered by Bresson who, in France, has to go back to the Scholastics for an aesthetic precedent and on the way forfeited any hope of mass popularity or commercial success.

Ozu's career was one of refinement: he constantly limited his technique, subject matter, and editorial comment. Early in his career (Ozu made fifty-four films over thirty-five years, from 1927 to 1962) he filmed the romantic and social themes insisted upon by Japanese producers, but later in life, particularly after the Second World War, Ozu limited himself to the *shomin* genre, and within the *shomin-geki* to certain forms of conflict and resolution.

The *shomin* genre concerns proletarian and middle-class life and "the sometimes humorous, sometimes bitter relations within the family."[6] The *shomin-geki*, initially a genre of melodrama and light comedy, originated in the later 1920s and early 30s, only after the Japanese middle class had become sufficiently entrenched to laugh at itself. Several critics have pointed out the evolution of Ozu's approach by comparing the 1932 *I Was Born, But . . . (Umarete Wa Mita Keredo)* with the 1959 remake, *Good Morning (Ohayo)*. Ozu's intentions in *I Was Born, But . . .* were social and particular; his intentions in *Good Morning* were satirical and universal. Compared to the remake, *I Was Born, But . . .* was "active rather than contemplative."[7] Ozu's early films (such as *I Was Born, But . . .*) were squarely within the original *shomin-geki* concept: light understated comedies with a tinge of social consciousness. Time, affluence, the war, governmental pressures, and Westernization sobered the *shomin-geki* in general, and Ozu in particular. When Ozu changed—when his light comedy slowly turned to "resigned sadness"—he took the *shomin-geki* with him, exerting much the same influence over the *shomin* genre as John Ford did over the American Western. Ozu's later films were not descriptive of the *shomin-geki*, but prescriptive of it.

"In every Ozu film," Richie writes, "the whole world exists in one family. The ends of the earth are no more distant than outside the house."[8] In his films the middle class is represented as office workers, and in some films, such as *Early Spring (Soshun, 1956)*, the office "family" replaces the household family unit. Ozu focuses on the tensions between the home and the office, the parent and the child, which are extensions of the tensions between the old and new Japan, between tradition and Westernization, and—ultimately—between man and nature.

Toward the end of his life (he died in 1963 at the age of sixty), Ozu focused his attention on certain forms of conflict within the *shomin-geki*. This conflict is not drama in Western terms, and it certainly is not plot: "Pictures with obvious plots bore me now," Ozu told Richie. "Naturally, a film must have some kind of structure or else it is not a film, but I feel that a picture isn't good if it has too much drama or action."[9] And concerning *Late Autumn (Akibiyori)*: "I want to portray a man's character by eliminating all the dramatic devices. I want to make people feel what life is like without delineating all the dramatic ups and downs."[10] In Ozu's mind Japanese life had resolved into certain opposing forces which he repeatedly demonstrated in his films, and although these forces must be reconciled, they would not be reconciled by anything as artificial as plot.

Tokyo Story: "In every Ozu film, the whole world exists in one family. The ends of the earth are no more distant than outside the house."

Ozu's later cycle of family-office films (thirteen films from 1949 to 1962) features the estrangement of parents and children. The incidents of estrangement are in themselves remarkably petty: marriage, relocation, bickerings, and at most running away from home. Behind these incidents are the divisive elements of modern Japan: the Second World War (the children are called the *après-guerre* generation) and Westernization (the compartmentalizing effect of office routine). The parent-child estrangement is not a failure to "communicate," as in American juvenile delinquency films. Even in successful relationships Ozu's characters do not communicate, as that word is used in sociological jargon, with commiseration and emotional interchange. The estrangement results from the loss of the traditional family unity which was never verbally communicated in the first place. In his later films Ozu set these opposing forces within a home-office superstructure containing a variety of interchangeable character-conflict infrastructures. One story (really nothing more than an anecdote) could sustain several films. Ozu was notorious for filming the same situation over and over again: the father-daughter conflict of *Late Spring* (*Banshun*, 1949) became the mother-daughter conflict of *Late Autumn* and reverted to a father-daughter conflict in *An Autumn Afternoon* (*Samma No Aji*, 1962).

Just as Ozu settled on certain conflicts to present in his films, he settled on certain people to help him present those conflicts. The majority of the later films were photographed by Yushun Atsuta and all were written in collaboration with Kogo Noda. Ozu and Noda enjoyed a legendary relationship between director and writer: "Although we don't write down the details of the sets, they are in our minds as one common image. We think alike. It is an amazing thing."[11] Ozu and Noda would devise the projected film entirely in their minds, word by word and image by image. After this extensive preparation (which took from four months to one year in seclusion), Ozu would mechanically shoot the preset Ozu-Noda script.

Similarly, Ozu settled on a select group of actors and actresses to appear in his films. The nucleus of this group consisted of Chishu Ryu, Setsuko Hara, Nobuo Nakamura, and Shin Saburi. They were Ozu's filmic "family." In each film they would play slight variations of character, acting out domestic conflicts with the sense of resigned awareness which comes from playing the same roles and feeling the same emotions many times. Ozu chose his actors not for their "star" quality or acting skill, but for their "essential" quality. "In casting it is not a matter of skillfulness or lack of skill an actor has. It is what he is. . . ."[12]

"The father-daughter conflict of *Late Spring* (left: Setsuko Hara, Chishu Ryu) became the mother-daughter conflict of *Late Autumn* (center: Hara, Yoko Tsukasa) and reverted to a father-daughter conflict in *An Autumn Afternoon* (right: Shima Iwashita, Ryu)."

But most of all, Ozu refined his technique. Ozu is cinema's consummate formalist; his films are characterized by "an abstentious rigor, a concern for brevity and economy, an aspiring to the ultimate in limitation."[13] Because Ozu's technique is so limited and predictable, it can be examined closely and in depth, a task which Donald Richie has accomplished in a remarkable article entitled, "Yasujiro Ozu: The Syntax of his Films."[14] Richie described Ozu's "syntax" as exemplified in his grammar, structure, editing, tempo, and scene, and there will be need to periodically refer to some of Richie's observations as this section progresses.

Ozu's camera is always at the level of a person seated in traditional fashion on the *tatami*, about three feet above the ground. "This traditional view is the view in repose, commanding a very limited field of vision. It is the attitude for watching, for listening, it is the position from which one sees the Noh, from which one partakes of the tea ceremony. It is the aesthetic attitude; it is the passive attitude."[15] The camera, except in the rarest of instances, never moves; in the later films there are no pans, no dollies, no zooms. Ozu's only filmic punctuation mark is the cut, and it is not the fast cut for impact or the juxtaposing cut for metaphorical meaning, but the pacing cut which denotes a steady, rhythmic succession of events.

One must not, however, mistake Ozu's "predictability" for superficiality or obviousness. It is not necessarily a virtue—nor necessarily a fault—if a director uses the same techniques repeatedly in film after film. Predictability in Ozu's films does not stem from a lack of initiative or originality, as it does in the films of some directors, but rather from the primitive concept of ritual in which repetition is preferred to variety.

It is possible to define Ozu's style by what it is not. Ozu is the film-maker who doesn't do certain things. This rarification of technique continued throughout Ozu's lifetime, from his first film to his last. As he got older there were more and more things he didn't do. This can be seen not only by comparing the early and later films (*I Was Born, But . . .* and *Good Morning*), but also by comparing the different phases of his later films. *Early Summer* (*Bakushu*, 1951) was made in about the middle of Ozu's later (postwar) period, yet it is markedly different from his last films made ten years later, *Late Autumn, The Autumn of the*

Kohayagawa Family (Kohayagawa-ke No Aki, 1961), and *An
Autumn Afternoon*. For example, in his last films Ozu completely
forsook certain techniques he had used in *Early Summer*: (1) the
tracking shot, of which there are fifteen in *Early Summer*, (2) a
closeup with emphasis on facial expression, such as an old man's
pleasure in watching the theatre, (3) a physical action to express
obvious emotion, such as the throwing down of a handkerchief
in disgust, (4) a cut on motion, that is, a cut which breaks one
action by an actor into two shots, (5) a cut between two different
indoor settings without an outdoor "coda" pause, (6) use of
chiaroscuro, non-"flat" lighting, although this is very rare even
in early Ozu. *Early Summer* also contains techniques which Ozu
did not completely discard but came to use less and less: (1)
nonfrontal (90°) angles, (2) camera takes of relatively short
duration, (3) scenes whose sole purpose was light comedy.

The purpose of this essay, however, is not to define Ozu's
style by what he omitted, but by what was left after his unceasing
prunings—his final style, which might be called a transcendental
style.

FOLLOWING THE FISH

Before one can analyze the transcendental style in Ozu's
films, one must make (or attempt to make) the crucial yet
elusive distinction between transcendental art and the art of
transcendental experience within Ozu's work. Do Ozu's films
express the Transcendent, or do they express Ozu, Zen culture,
and man's experience of the Transcendent?

The first, immediate answer must be: "both, of course."
There is no static-free communication with the Holy and any
work which expresses the Transcendent must also express
the personality and culture of its artist. Then comes the thorny
problem of individual instances, of determining influences and
effects. The distinction between transcendental art and the art
of transcendental experience resolves into several incumbent
questions: which influenced Ozu's art more? His personality,*

---

* A belated definition of "personality" may be helpful at this juncture.
"Personality," as used in this essay, refers to those psychological
characteristics which distinguish one person from another, such as his
preoccupations, needs, likes, dislikes, idiosyncrasies. It does not refer to
those subconscious, archetypal characteristics in which all men are similar.

Zen culture, or the Transcendent? And which critical definition of style is best suited to uncover that influence? The personal, cultural, or Eliade-Wolfflin (transcendental style)?

All three critical methods reveal something about Ozu's films, and none can be neglected. Each can best reveal its respective influence. But for every artist there is an appropriate priority of critical methods, an artist's personality may be a reflection of his surroundings, or vice versa. In Ozu's films it seems that his personality was enveloped by Zen culture, and that Zen culture was enveloped by a transcending reality, like the fish who ate the fish who ate the fish. And, tracing this sequence of influences, it is hoped one will arrive at the final unique influence on Ozu and his films.

Ozu and His Personality

The question of personality is not simply a matter of whether or not it is possible to detect Ozu's personality in his films. Obviously it is. The dilemmas and solutions of Ozu's films are also the dilemmas and solutions of his own life. Ozu never married, but stayed at home living with his aging mother. His films are often about the relationships of children to parents, the hard decisions of marriage, and the trauma of the family "breaking up." Following this critical emphasis, one writer has contended that the mother is stronger in Ozu's films because she was so in his own life.[16] As is often the case with film-makers, the age of Ozu's lead character usually corresponded to his own age, and as Ozu grew older his characters came more and more to embody the older traditional virtues of Japan. On the other hand, there were also many experiences in Ozu's life which he did not represent on film. (His experiences as an army sergeant and a newspaperman are not reflected in his films to any appreciable degree.)

It might be more helpful to phrase the question of Ozu's personality differently. To what extent was Ozu's personality unique, and to what extent was it representative of the Zen culture? Did Ozu subjugate his personality in the manner of the traditional Oriental artist, or were his films actually highly individualistic expressions? Post-Renaissance Western art, including motion pictures, has been structured, by and large, around the concept of personal expression—"the delusion,"

Coomaraswamy says, "that I am the doer"—whereas in traditional Oriental art "human individuality is not an end but only a means."[17] If Ozu was a "personal" director like, say, Fellini (that is, if he sought primarily to express his personality in his films), that would seem to place him in the tradition of Western individualistic art rather than traditional Oriental art.

Richie seems to ride both sides of the issue: on one hand he writes that "Ozu is not an intuitive artist, he is a master craftsman; for him, film is not expression but function,"[18] and on the other hand he states that Ozu's approach is "intuitive rather than analytic."[19] Questioned about the apparent contradiction of his statements Richie replied, "Ozu was a craftsman who always made his films the same way. He never varied his way of making a film, nor his way of editing one—a long and painful process. Now this means that he was a craftsman. But I don't think he ever thought of what all this *meant*—and in that regard I find him intuitive. He did what he felt like doing. Ozu would talk with you for hours about a kind of lens of a certain color, but if you asked about the meaning of anything or the idea behind his presented idea he would shut up. He wasn't interested. Ozu's inner self is there for all to see, but my point is that showing it was not one of his concerns."[20] And later, "I think that my riding both sides of the matter is correct and I think it is the only position to take in a non-dualistic culture."[21]

On closer examination one realizes that Richie's fence-straddling is unavoidable, and, as he says, proper. The personal versus cultural dilemma which so vexes Western critics would not have occurred to the traditional Oriental artist. Considered in the larger context of Zen culture, man and his surroundings are counterenveloping, just as are mind and body, content and form; any distinction between them is arbitrary. If Ozu's work is really steeped in Zen culture, as the next section maintains, then any study of the "individual" Yasujiro Ozu apart from traditional Zen values is meaningless. To compound the paradox one might say that Ozu's intuition was nonintuitive, that is, his instincts were formalistic. This may strike the Westerner as a meaningless contradiction, and it is a natural roadblock to any cross-cultural appreciation of Ozu's films in particular or traditional Oriental art in general. Because Zen is a cultural phenomenon (that is, it occurs within a particular area among a particular number of people), it is possible to say that the Zen culture envelopes the individual personality, but none of these statements, including paradoxical epigrams like "Ozu's intuition was nonintuitive," have any meaning until one realizes that both personality and culture are enveloped by a transcending reality.

It is possible to detect Ozu's personal life and beliefs in his films, but this does not mean that the personality-oriented critical method is the best approach to his films. The privileged information garnered from his private life may be irrelevant. If we happened to know a great deal about the private life of Zen artist Ma Yuan it would not explain his "one-corner" style of *sumi-e* painting; similarly, all the facts of Ozu's private life cannot explain his mysterious transcendental pauses. These elements are not derived from an individual personality.

The personal interpretation of Ozu's films has been encouraged by two misleading circumstances: one, that we simply happen to know much more about Ozu than we do about earlier traditional artists, and two, that Ozu, unlike a Zen poet or painter, must use living human beings as his raw material. The characters on screen are experiencing life, and the critic, who naturally empathizes with their feelings, may conclude that their feelings are representative of the film-maker and let the matter go at that. But the characters who are emoting on screen may be no more or less representative of the film-maker than a nonhuman shot of a train or a building. The characters' individual feelings (sorrow, joy, introspection) are of passing importance: it is the surrounding form which gives them lasting value. Each person, each emotion is part of a larger form which is not an experience at all, but an expression, or rather, not an expression of the individual or cultural experience of transcendence, but an expression of the Transcendent itself.

Every indication is that Ozu did not attempt to explore his personality through the psychology of his characters. On the contrary, he made every attempt to drain his actors of any psychological nuance, any emotion. Ozu's actors report that he would force them to do the same scene twenty or thirty consecutive times until any hint of nuance or subtlety had been frozen into rote, automaton-like action, and only then would he approve the scene for final shooting. Actors were forbidden to make even natural actions if these disturbed Ozu's composition. These circumstances, and many others like them, seem to indicate that Ozu was after a bigger prize than personal, psychological revelation, that he sought, like the traditional Oriental artist, to eliminate his personality in order to propose a thesis.

BEYOND PERSONALITY: OZU AND ZEN CULTURE

Much of Ozu's approach is derived from Japanese culture itself, and it is the traditional elements which make him the "most Japanese of all directors." The most appropriate analogy for the cultural elements in Ozu's films is Zen art. Zen is not an organized religion with physical and political concerns like Shintoism or Christianity, but a way of living which has permeated the fabric of Japanese culture. The Allied Powers' Religious and Cultural Division reported: "The type of conduct usually expressed by the words 'Japanese spirit' is essentially Zen in nature,"[22] a conclusion echoed by both Alan Watts[23] and Langdon Warner.[24] Zen is the quintessence of traditional Japanese art, an art which Ozu sought to introduce into cinema. In Japanese history the way of Zen came to predominate in certain arts—painting, gardening, the tea ceremony, poetry, archery, Noh drama, Judo, Kendo—and these arts are the precedents for Ozu's films. Tom Milne has written that Ozu's films are structured like the haiku with its pauses and pregnant statements,[25] but the haiku, of course, is only one example of an attitude in all the Zen arts and in Ozu's films.

Perhaps the basic principle of Zen art is the first *koan* of Zen, *mu*, the concept of negation, emptiness, and void. Emptiness, silence, and stillness are positive elements in Zen art, and represent presence rather than the absence of something. "The blank sheet of paper is perceived only as paper, and remains as paper," Will Peterson writes. "Only by filling the paper does it become empty. Much in the same way the sound of the frog plopping into the still pond creates the silence in Basho's well-known haiku. The sound gives form to the silence—the emptiness."[26] *Mu* is the character used to refer to the spaces between the branches of a flower arrangement; the emptiness is an integral part of the form. Ma Yuan, Sung painter and originator of the "one-corner style," painted only one corner of

Ma Yüan, *Lone Fisherman*, the "one-corner style":
"The blank sheet of paper is perceived only as paper, and remains as paper. Only by filling the paper, does it become empty."

the canvas, leaving the remainder blank. The emptiness, however, was a part of the painting and not just an unpainted background. The simple fishing boat placed in one corner gives meaning to the whole space. In the same manner the stones in a Zen garden give meaning to the raked space, and the lines of a haiku give meaning to the unwritten transitions.

Like the traditional Zen artist, Ozu directs silences and voids. Silence and emptiness are active ingredients in Ozu's films; characters respond to them as if they were audible sounds and tangible objects. Although such responses are usually quite subtle, a rather obvious use of active silence occurs in *Early Summer*: Setsuko Hara has just told her parents of her intention to marry, a decision which displeases them. After a polite argument the parents, despondent, go upstairs. In the next shot the father is staring into the camera while in the background the mother does some busywork and speaks to him. She makes a trivial remark, and he replies, "Ah." She makes another remark, he again replies, "Ah." The mother leaves the room and Hara walks noiselessly through the background. The father again says, "Ah." The silence has become electric, much more meaningful than anything the mother could have said.

In Ozu's films it is also possible to detect a remnant of the thirteenth-century one-corner style. A static environment fills

Ozu's frame while in one corner a distant action (boats, trains
slowly moving, people conversing) occurs. In *The Flavor of
Green Tea Over Rice (Ochazuke No Aji,* 1952) there is an
obvious example of this: the husband has just left for a lengthy
stay in South America. His wife, who had inexplicably left home
several days earlier, did not come to the airport to see him off.
As his plane departs Ozu holds it in the upper right-hand corner
of the frame. The rest of the frame is empty, and the plane slowly
vanishes from view. It is a "full" composition, and as in the
one-corner paintings, the plane brings out the quality of the void.

But most of all, *mu* is expressed in Ozu's "codas." His
films are structured between action and emptiness, between
indoors and outdoors, between scene and coda. The conflicts are
always explicated in indoors, usually in long dispassionate
conversations. The settings may vary (home, office, bar,
restaurant), but the story is rarely forwarded by anything but
indoor conversations (and the one or two exceptions in each film
are thematically crucial). These indoor discussions are set off
by "codas": still-life scenes of outdoor Japanese life, empty
streets and alleys, a passing train or boat, a distant mountain or
lake. Richie has described Ozu's films as a combination of (1)
long shots, (2) medium shots, (3) close-ups, in the usual sequence
of 1-2-3-2-1.[27] The coda still-life shots are inserted between the
long shots, thus linking the conversational indoor by outdoor
still lifes. Each of the codas sets off an Ozu "paragraph," to use
Richie's terminology. There are no chapters, only paragraphs
and codas. The codas in Ozu's films fulfill the same purpose as
the *mu* between the stones in the famous Ryōan-ji garden: "the
emptiness is that of desertion. Man is implied, but is not present,
and the resultant sensation is one of longing and loneliness."[28] In
Western art one would naturally assume that the codas are
inserted to give weight to the paragraphs, but for Ozu, as for
Zen, it is precisely the opposite: the dialogue gives meaning to
the silence, the action to the still life. Ozu is permeated with *mu*;
it is the single character inscribed on his tomb at Engaku-ji.

"When life is empty," Watts writes, "with respect to the
past, and aimless with respect to the future, the vacuum is filled
with the present."[29] In Zen art the sense of the "infinitely
expanded present" is nowhere stronger than in the art of tea
(*cha-no-yu*). The tea ceremony celebrates the present tense

Ozu's codas: above, a train passing a clothesline in *Tokyo Story;* below, the mountain in *Late Autumn.* "One would naturally assume that the still life codas are inserted to give weight to the action, but for Ozu, as for Zen, it is the opposite: the action gives meaning to the still life."

through a meticulously predetermined ritual. In the sixteenth century as many as one hundred rules for *cha-no-yu* were laid down, determining everything from the subjects to be discussed during tea to the depth of the lacquer on the tea caddy. Rather than occupy the mind, these minute rules free it, enabling it to think of nothing, to be timeless, or in the words of a famous Zenrin poem, to be "sitting quietly, doing nothing."

Similarly, Ozu's films portray the "aimless, self-sufficient eternal now" (*ekaksana*). "His characters . . . are living in the *now*," Richie writes, "and they have no history . . . when a person dies in Ozu's world (which is often) he is merely and instantly *gone*. There are no ghosts in Ozu as there are in Resnais and Bergman. The past barely exists for Ozu."[30] "Nostalgia" in Ozu's films, such as the scene when the father in *An Autumn Afternoon* revisits the bar where the barmaid resembles his dead wife, is not so much a longing for the past in Western terms but is more likely an "expansion" of the present so familiar to Zen art. When Ozu focuses on a wall clock, watching the seconds tick futilely away, it is partially to contrast film time and psychological time, as both Milne and Richie suggest, but it is also to create the mood of total timelessness integral to Zen art. The clock is impotent; mechanical time does not affect those living in an eternal present. There is no "race against the clock." A shot of a clock serves the same purpose as, say, a shot of a vase; its movements are not those of time, but the imperceptible movements of the mind in contemplation. Ozu importantly includes the clock shots in his codas; time is part of the *mu*, the nothingness.

Ozu achieves the "eternal now" in the same manner as *cha-no-yu*, through ritual. Each possible event in an Ozu film can be reduced to a predetermined, limited and precise number of shots. If the tea bowl is of a certain color or texture, a certain type of conversation will ensue; if an Ozu character is in a certain location, a certain type of conversation will ensue. In the home Ozu characters discuss domestic arrangements (finances, housework, what other family members are doing); at the office they make concrete arrangements (future meeting places and times); in a restaurant they reminisce and discuss social problems (marriage proposals, what other members of the family

The Flavor of Green Tea Over Rice.
Ozu's four locations: the restaurant, office, home and bar. "If an Ozu
character is in a certain location, a certain type of conversation
will ensue."

are doing); in a bar they reminisce and express disillusionment
(the *après-guerre* generation, office life). These categorizations
are not ironclad, but neither is the tea ceremony; they are
products of what Zen calls "controlled accident."

In Zen painting the technique ritual evolved into an
alphabet of brush strokes. There were a certain number of brush
strokes used to represent natural objects; they were learned
by rote, practiced piecemeal, and were meaningless until
assembled. Similarly one may speak of Ozu's alphabet, a set of
predetermined shots from which he would never depart. Just
as a Zen painter would use the "crab claw" stroke to represent a
bunch of pine needles, so Ozu would use a shot of a clothesline
in the foreground and a moving train in the background to

express the feeling of permanence within transience (*mono no aware*). In traditional Oriental art these would be practiced to perfection; an artist would spend his life perfecting certain brush strokes, painting and repainting the same scene. Ozu was also a perfectionist; he spent his life perfecting a small repertoire of shots, filming and refilming the same story. The end product of a Zen painter's career could be a single painting; similarly, the end product of Ozu's career can be described as a single film.

In a Zen artistic alphabet—whether in painting, gardening, or the tea ceremony—the same letter is never repeated identically within one work. A difference, however minute, is always inserted between two items which may seem to be identical. This may be a variation of brush stroke in a calligraphic letter, or a slight deviation in parallel architectural structures. Even in such nearly indiscernible matters Ozu adheres to the tradition of Zen art. Although it is possible in film, unlike any other art, to have photographic identicality, Ozu repudiates it. When repeating the same letter of his filmic alphabet, say, a shot of Chishu Ryu walking down the street in front of his home, Ozu would film each letter/shot separately. To the unpracticed eye it may seem as if Ozu has reprinted one shot over and over, using it a dozen times in one film, but each shot is a separate entity and there is variety within seeming repetition.

Ritual in Oriental art is not structured around a single cathartic event (like the blinding of Oedipus, for instance), but is cyclic, with little rise and fall, revealing the timeless Oneness of man and nature. "Where European art naturally depicts a moment in time," Coomaraswamy writes, "an arrested action or an effect of light, Oriental art represents a continuous continuation."[31] The continuation is based on the infrastructure of ritual. A certain pattern of shots is repeatable within an Ozu paragraph, a certain pattern of Ozu paragraphs is repeatable within an Ozu film, and a certain number of Ozu films are repeatable within an Ozu career. The ritual is not separate from the form, which is not separate from the content.

In Ozu's films, as in all traditional Oriental art, the form itself is the ritual which creates the eternal present (*ekaksana*), gives weight to the emptiness (*mu*), and makes it possible to evoke the *furyu*, the four basic untranslatable moods of Zen which are described thus by Watts:

Where the mood of the moment is solitary and quiet it is called *sabi*. When the artist is feeling depressed or sad, and this peculiar emptiness of feeling catches a glimpse of something rather ordinary and unpretentious in its incredible "suchness," the mood is called *wabi*. When the moment evokes a more intense, nostalgic sadness connected with autumn and the vanishing away of the world, it is called *aware*. And when the vision is the hinting at an unknown never to be discovered, the mood is called *yugen*.[32]

Although each of the *furyu* are obviously present in Ozu's films, Richie writes that Ozu is primarily the artist of *mono no aware* for which he gives Tamako Niwa's translation, "sympathetic sadness": "the end effect of an Ozu film is a kind of resigned sadness, a calm and knowing serenity which maintains despite the uncertainty of life and the things of this world."[33] Ozu's technique, Richie writes elsewhere, is saturated with *wabi* because of its poverty and "extraordinary restriction."[34] It is very difficult for the average Western viewer to appreciate the *aware* of Ozu's themes or the *wabi* of his technique, much less to distinguish between the moods of the *furyu*. The Japanese-English dictionary itself despairs of any attempt to define or delimit the aesthetic twins of *sabi* and *wabi*. Simply because the Western viewer cannot make the distinctions between *sabi, wabi, aware,* and *yugen* in Ozu's films he should not mistakenly think that Ozu is after a single basic emotion, as is much of Western psychological realism. The codas of Ozu's films are remarkably complex, and the difference between a still shot of a vase, a *tatami*, and Mount Fuji may mean the difference between *sabi, wabi,* and *aware*. When the still shot of the vase is first shown in *Late Spring* it evokes *wabi*, but by the time that same shot is "repeated" later in the film it also connotes both *aware* and *yugen*.

The fountainhead of Zen and Zen art is a fundamental unity of experience—"all things are of one Suchness." Any dichotomy between man and nature (which Zen scholar D. T. Suzuki defines as, "all that constitutes what is commonly known as man's objective world"[35]) is false. When Yahweh set Adam over the Garden of Eden he set the West on a course that the East has never accepted. "I am Nature and Nature is me," Suzuki wrote. "Not mere participation in each other, but a fundamental identity between the two."[36] Translated into Western terms this comes close to pantheism, a comparison Zen would not accept because pantheism involves an artificial conceptualization of a unity which is natural and spontaneous. The unity of man and nature finds pure expression in the Zen garden. When a Zen priest ceaselessly clips, prunes, weeds, and trains his garden "he is not interfering with Nature because he is Nature."[37] In its most reactionary form (at least to Western minds) this unity is expressed in the analogy that as the fish swims in the water and never wearies of it, so man lives in nature and should never tire of it.

The greatest conflict (and the greatest resulting disillusionment) in Ozu's films is not political, psychological, or domestic, but is, for want of a better term, "environmental." That the aged cannot communicate with the young, that the parents cannot communicate with their children, that the craftsmen cannot communicate with the office workers—these are all dimensions of the problem that the modern Japanese cannot communicate with his environment. During a disillusioning saké-drinking bout a character in *Late Autumn* says, "It is people who tend to complicate life. Life itself is very simple." This despair is reflected in a similar drinking scene in *Early Spring* in which a character says, "The world today isn't very interesting," and his friend replies, "That's the fate that is awaiting us. Just disillusionment and loneliness." These statements reflect a breakdown in the traditional attitude toward nature in Zen art. How can man complicate life? How can the fish complicate the water? This for Ozu, is the great threat of modernization: it threatens the traditional Oneness, and when that unity wobbles the rest of the structures—home, office— come tumbling after. This real or potential disunity between man and nature has always been a theme of Japanese art but has gained a certain schizoid intensity since "modernization" in Japan. The affront of *après-guerre* Japanese youth (and it is extraordinarily mild in Ozu compared to younger directors like Hani and Oshima) against parents and political leaders is an extension of their affront against the traditional concepts of acceptance and "flowing."

Ozu responds to the disunity in Japanese life by evoking

the traditional verities of Zen art in a contemporary, cinematic context. He is naturally more predisposed to the older generation because they are closer to traditional culture and because time itself evokes *aware,* the mood of autumn. "I am somewhat more sympathetic with the old people than with the young," Ozu stated in 1958. "The theme of many recent movies tends to deny the values of the old generation and to approve of the erratic behavior of the young. But the old people are displeased by the aimless rebellion of the young and are apt to oppose them."[38] In the tradition of Zen art, Ozu does not forge an artificial synthesis between the old and the young, man and nature, but situates these elements within the larger context of the *furyu* which affects and encompasses everything. The runaway, *après-guerre* daughter of *Tokyo Twilight (Tokyo Boshoku,* 1957) manifests the same "sympathetic sadness" which permeates her respectable, misunderstanding father. *The Flavor of Green Tea Over Rice* is one of the least successful of Ozu's later films because he breaks his rule of situating seeming conflicts within the larger context of the *furyu.* Ozu normally resolves the conflict between parent and child by demonstrating that, no matter what their personal differences are, both share a deep sense of *mono no aware.* In *Green Tea,* however, Ozu attempts to portray a change of heart, a conversion from coldness to *aware,* rather than, as in his other films, a gradual understanding that *aware* was always present. As a result, the wife's "conversion" is quite unconvincing and Ozu resorts to a rare use of gimmick (the husband's plane is forced to return because of bad weather) to make his point. The wife's "change of heart" violates the Zen belief that unity is always present, and that all man need do is become cognizant of it. There cannot be a "conversion" because that would imply that there had been a change—that where there once had been disunity there is now unity—which would violate the principal that there never had been a disunity. Ozu was probably conscious of the error of *Green Tea;* he never again attempted such a drastic change of character and once admitted that *Green Tea* was "not well made."[39]

Because of Ozu's normal emphasis on unity rather than disunity, on *aware* rather than conflict, he is not really the advocate of either the old or the young, but the advocate of

The final coda for *Tokyo Story*: "The final codas of Ozu's films are reaffirmations of nature; they are the final silence and emptiness."

traditional Oneness: "His films so faithfully reflect Japanese life that—more than any other director—Ozu is the spokesman for both the older and younger generations."[40]

The final shots of Ozu's films, like the codas, are reaffirmations of nature. These shots may depict something as traditional as a mountain, or it may incorporate such contemporary elements as a boat on a river, or a smokestack. These scenes are the final codas, the final silences and emptiness. Ozu does not eliminate the conflict between man and nature by plot maneuverings or psychological revelations, but by merging man and nature with Zen thought and life. He does not so much eliminate the conflict between man and nature as, you might say, he transcends it.

Zen art and culture is an accurate metaphor for Ozu's films. Other precedents can be found for Ozu's techniques: the rote repetition of movement was a gag in Japanese silent comedy and became incorporated into Ozu's technique; and his stationary camera shots, Ozu once half-facetiously stated, were due to the fact that a dolly could not operate at such a low angle. And, of course, his "personality" also influenced his approach to film-making. But taken as a whole Ozu's techniques are so similar to traditional Zen methods that the influence is unmistakable, and one must consequently assume that Ozu's personality, like that of the traditional artist, is only valuable to the extent that it expresses his thesis. His personality, like those of his characters, merges with an enveloping sense of *mono no aware*, and—the ultimate achievement of Zen art— finally becomes undistinguishable from it.

Beyond Zen Culture: the Transcendental Style

Ozu instilled the virtues of Zen art into motion pictures and in the process he utilized certain elements which were not necessarily limited to Japanese culture, but which can also be found in France, Denmark, Italy, the United States and wherever else artists try to express the Transcendent in motion pictures. These are the common qualities of transcendental style and take the form of three progressive steps. This section will attempt to extricate these steps from Ozu's films, and the next chapter, on Bresson, will discuss their component parts and the possible effects on the viewer more precisely. One cannot analyze the transcendental style from the perspective of a single culture (e.g., Zen) or it might seem to be an exclusive product of that culture. One must study the steps of this style as used by different artists in different cultures to ascertain its truly universal qualities. One can extract the transcendental style from Zen culture but the test of its universality will rest on its use elsewhere.

The desire of Ozu, Bresson, and to lesser degrees, Dreyer and others to express the *aware*, ideal or ecstatic (not synonymous terms, but all transcendent) is formalized in the triad of transcendental style, and it is perhaps not coincidental that these steps correspond to the classic Zen aphorism: "When I began to study Zen, mountains were mountains; when I thought I understood Zen, mountains were not mountains; but when I came to full knowledge of Zen, mountains were again mountains." The steps of transcendental style are:

1. *The everyday: a meticulous representation of the dull, banal commonplaces of everyday living,* or what Ayfre quotes Jean Bazaine as calling *"le quotidien."*[41]

At one time such an approach would have been called "realism," but it is more accurately a stylization. The desire to strip life of all expression often bypasses the reality of day-to-day living which, after all, does have moments of genuine theater and melodrama. Given a selection of inflections, the choice is monotone; a choice of sounds, the choice is silence; a selection of actions, the choice is stillness—there is no question of "reality." It is obvious why a transcendental artist in cinema (the "realistic" medium) would choose such a representation of life: it prepares reality for the intrusion of the Transcendent, much in the way that *cha-no-yu* prepares tea drinking for any of the moods of the *furyu*. The everyday celebrates the bare threshold of existence, those banal occurrences which separate the living from the dead, the physical from the material, those occurrences which so many people equate with life itself. The everyday meticulously sets up the straw man of day-to-day reality (the illusion that the mountain is only a mountain *materially*), so that it may be knocked down later.

Many artists have used "realism" as a springboard for other interpretations of life, overlaying a seemingly realistic environment with fantasy, folk-myth, expressionism, and so forth. Carried to the extreme, this tendency to create an underminable reality results in the everyday. Most of these artificial "realities" are designed with built-in loopholes which the film-maker can conveniently slip through later in the film. For example, because the grim "realism" of Buñuel's *Los Olvidados* bristles with volatile emotions it is not surprising later in the film when those emotions pass the borderline into fantasy. This is not to fault Buñuel's film, but only to point out that his prefantasy "realism" is not the everyday. The everyday attempts to close up all those loopholes; it rejects all the biased interpretations of reality, even if they are such conventionally acceptable "realistic" techniques as characterization, multiple point-of-view camerawork, telltale sound effects. In the everyday nothing is expressive, all is coldness.

The opening five shots of *An Autumn Afternoon*: "The everyday celebrates the bare threshold of existence; it meticulously sets up the straw man of day-to-day reality."

In Ozu, the stylization is near complete. Every shot is from the same height, every composition static, every conversation monotone, every expression bland, every cut forthright and predictable. No action is intended as a comment on another, no event leads inexorably to the next. The highpoints of conventional drama, the beginning and the end, are neglected.

The "action" usually occurs in the middle of a scene; a setting is established, there is an expectation that something will occur, a conversation takes place, a line or two seems to have some importance but the conversation passes over them, the discussion trails off unsatisfied and unfulfilled, the people exit, and the image draws to a close. By placing the action in the middle ground (Bresson uses this technique for as simple a matter as opening a door; in Boetticher it encompasses the whole story) the action is deprived of its cathartic meaning, set into the "flow" of life, and again stylized. Every aspect of Ozu's film-making— storyline, acting, camera-work, soundtrack—falls under the tight restriction of the everyday, and the exact techniques of this restriction, though perhaps already apparent, will be discussed in connection with Bresson's use of everyday.

If the everyday was an end in itself it would be a style rather than as a step within a style. As such the everyday artist would see life as totally deprived of meaning, expression, drama or cathartic, as in Warhol's early films. But as part of the transcendental style, the everyday is clearly a prelude to the moment of redemption, when ordinary reality is transcended.

2. *Disparity: an actual or potential disunity between man and his environment which culminates in a decisive action;* what Jean Sémolué calls *"un moment décisif"* when writing of Bresson's films.[42]

This disparity is a growing crack in the dull surface of everyday reality, and, if one were restricted to Fretag's triangle, it might be described as the inciting incident. This step casts suspicion on the nonemotional everyday; the viewer suspects that there might be more to life than day-to-day existence, that the mountain may in fact not be a mountain. This creates a schizoid reaction in the viewer; the first step negated his emotions, told him they were of no use, and yet in the second step he begins to feel that all is not right in this banal world. He is in a mood of expectation; he seeks direction as to what role his feelings will play.

Disparity is caused by the insertion of what Ayfre calls "human density" into the cold context of the everyday. "The illusion of the reality of transcendent values depends upon the presence of a minimum of reality of human values," Ayfre wrote. "The 'fabulous,' if it is to be anything more than an abstract pattern of allegories or meaningless juggling, needs a human density."[43] In films of transcendental style there is, in this stage, an inexplicable outpouring of human feeling which can have no adequate receptacle. This overwhelming compassion seems *sui generis*, it comes suddenly and unexpectedly and is not derived from the empirically observed environment. If a human being can have true and tender feelings within an unfeeling environment, then there must necessarily be a disparity between man and environment. If the environment is unfeeling, where do man's feelings come from?

Examined more closely, however, this "human density" is actually a spiritual density. This boundless compassion is more than any human can bear and more than any human can receive. This compassion is marked by solemnity and suffering; it is an extension of the holy agony. Such overwhelming compassion cannot come from the cold environment or the humane instinct, but comes only from touching the transcendent ground of being. It is a totally out-of-place emotion, a burden rather than a tool in dealing with an unfeeling environment. The "growing crack in the dull surface of everyday reality" becomes an open rupture, and finally, in the moment of decisive action, there is an outburst of spiritual emotion totally inexplicable within the everyday.

During disparity the spectator watches agonizing human feelings and experiences on screen; there is no expression of the Transcendent. Instead, there is only a totally unresolved tension between a maximum of human expression and nonexpression. Disparity extends spiritual schizophrenia—that acute sense of two opposing worlds—to the viewer.

A potential disparity between man and nature underlies Ozu's films. He suggests that the flow of man and nature may be separate rather than unified, which, within the context of his traditional structure, certainly does create a schizoid reaction. This disparity becomes obvious when Ozu juxtaposes similar codas after contrasting family scenes. A shot of a snow-capped mountain inserted after a discussion by several parents plainly suggests the unity to which they aspire, but the same shot inserted after a parent-child quarrel suggests that the traditional unity may have little meaning within the postwar family structure. The codas cannot only be a positive statement on the unity of man and nature, but also a wry commentary on the lack of it.

For the most part, disparity in Ozu's films is conveyed by a strange human density which seems inappropriate to the clinically observed environment, and which, at the moment of decisive action, reveals itself to be a spiritual weight. Throughout his films there is an undercurrent of compassion which, although not overtly expressed, seems inherent in the treatment of the characters by each other and more importantly by their director. The viewer senses that there are deep, untapped feelings just below the surface. Usually this "sense" of compassion is nothing obvious, it is not tied into dialogue or editorial camera techniques, but is a matter of camera nuance. Tadao Sato, a Japanese critic, points out one example of this: in *Late Spring* the aunt and her niece are seated in front of their home bidding farewell to a guest. Ozu shoots the scene in his conventional manner—a perpendicular single angle showing the ladies bowing and putting their hands on the *tatami*. But then the ladies suddenly break the timing and balance so basic to Ozu's technique and the upper parts of their bodies swing clumsily out of balance, one to the right, the other to the left. This is a trifling movement, one often seen in natural life, but in the context of Ozu's strict everyday it brings an unexpected flash of human density. "In the picture of strict geometrical balance," Sato writes, "it sometimes happens that the movement of a man is made to feel very fresh by letting us see the movement which delicately breaks the balance."[44]

In a similarly ambivalent manner Ozu simultaneously evokes both laughter at and sympathy for his characters. Even when he makes fun of his characters, as in the drinking scene in *Tokyo Story* (*Tokyo Monogatori*, 1953), Ozu also evokes sympathy for them. His unblinking camera impresses the viewer with its fairness, its willingness to watch all of a man's conduct, both ludicrous and noble, without comment. The director seems to have compassion for his characters, he respects even their most fatuous feelings, yet also seems to be an objective observer. The characters seem to be automatons, yet they also seem to have periodic, natural human gestures. The nagging sense of disparity grows and grows.

Chieko Higashiyama and Setsuko Hara in *Tokyo Story*: the irony of disparity. "What a treat to sleep on my dead son's bed."

In this mild form disparity is often reflected by a thoroughgoing sense of irony. In films of transcendental style, irony is the temporary solution to living in a schizoid world. The principal characters take an attitude of detached awareness, find humor in the bad as well as the good, passing judgment on nothing. The characters treat life with irony and are in turn treated with irony by their directors. Ironic humor is obviously present in the films of Bresson, Dreyer, and Boetticher, but it is also present in the films of Ozu. In *Tokyo Story* the grandmother expresses the ironic mode perfectly when she says to her widowed daughter-in-law, "What a treat to sleep on my dead son's bed." But later in the same film she herself is treated with irony: the grandfather watches from a distance as the grandmother asks their young grandson what he will be when he grows up, but the grandson ignores her, running playfully away. In *An Autumn Afternoon* the ironical situations are reversed: first two friends, Kawei and Hirayama, play a joke on a waitress (and the audience) by straightforwardly pretending that their third companion, Professor Horei, has suddenly died of too much lovemaking; later in the film Kawei and Horei play a similar joke on Hirayama (and the audience) by pretending that the arrangements for his daughter's marriage have fallen through. The humor in each scene is malicious by normal standards,[45] but because Ozu's characters take an ironical attitude toward life, such jokes are passed off as light humor. Irony is Ozu's way to cope with disparity—in lieu of transcendence.

Ozu's use of character ambivalence and irony is similar to that of Czech director Milos Forman, and an interesting comparison can be drawn between their films. Both perfected a form of light comedy which contrasted documentary "realism" with flashes of human density. In their comedies, disparity is reflected by a tragicomic attitude toward character and a resultant irony. Their early films, given cultural differences, were remarkably similar, but Ozu's later films moved gradually out of the light comedy category and acquired a weight as yet unknown to Forman's work. This is because the later Ozu films employ transcendental style: by changing superficial "realism" to the rigid everyday and by changing mild disparity (character ambivalence, irony) into unexpected decisive action, Ozu transforms human density into spiritual density. Assuming that Forman and Ozu started from an analogous base in light comedy (*Black Peter* vis-à-vis *I Was Born, But* . . .), Ozu's evolution may be hypothesized thus: the twin influences of the age of postwar Westernization heightened the innate conflict between Zen culture and modernization in Ozu and forced him little by little to intensify his already schizoid style so that the differences could no longer be resolved but had to be transcended. The compassion of Ozu's later films is so overburdening and disparate that rapprochement cannot be achieved by laughter as in light comedy, but only by a deep spiritual awareness. (Milos Forman is still a young director, of course, although the surrealistic conclusion of *Firemen's Ball* suggests that his career will take a different course.)

Disparity, therefore, is a gradual process, each progressive step eating away at the solid veneer of everyday reality. At first, it is a "sense" of compassion which teases the viewer, making him believe that emotions are present but giving him no tangible proof. Finally, it is a *decisive action*, a totally bold call for emotion which dismisses any pretense of everyday reality. The decisive action breaks the everyday stylization; it is an incredible event within the banal reality which must by and large be taken on faith. In its most drastic form, as in Dreyer's *Ordet*, this decisive action is an actual miracle, the raising of the dead. In its less drastic forms, it is still somewhat miraculous: a nonobjective, emotional event within a factual, emotionless environment. The technical stops employed by the everyday are to varying degrees pulled out—the music soars, the characters emote. The everyday denigrated the viewer's emotions, showing they were of no use, disparity first titillates those emotions, suggesting that there might be a place for them, and then in the decisive action suddenly and inexplicably demands the viewer's full emotional output. How the viewer reacts to this demand by and large determines to what extent the final step of transcendental style, stasis, will be achieved.

The decisive actions in Ozu's films are less dramatic and less obvious than in the films of Bresson or Dreyer. In an Ozu film there are likely to be several preludial decisive actions before the culminant one. In *An Autumn Afternoon*, for example, each coda is a small decisive action—a burst of four-directional Western music demands an emotional output when there is nothing on the screen but a still-life view to receive it. In addition, there are three scenes in which the codas are combined with tears: the spinster daughter of a noodle-shop owner breaks down in tears when her father is brought home drunk, Hirayama's daughter cries when she discovers that the young man of her choice is already married, and at the conclusion of the film Hirayama himself weeps silently after his daughter has been married. In each case the person weeps alone; it is not a public spectacle, but an outpouring of their deepest emotions. The weeping here, like Setsuko Hora's famous tears at the conclusion of *Tokyo Story*, is plausible but unexpected —the viewer has seemingly not been prepared for such an emotional outburst. In *An Autumn Afternoon* every other event has been accepted with complete stoicism; even when Kawei and Horei play their "malicious" joke on Hirayama, he only nods resignedly. Except in these rare, "decisive" moments irony and the everyday prevent any display of emotion.

Of the culminant decisive action, Hirayama's solitary weeping, Tom Milne writes, "Nothing, apparently, has prepared for the emotional depth of the last scene, yet it is a perfectly natural climax towards which the whole film has been moving."[46] Throughout *An Autumn Afternoon* Hirayama had been a paragon of stoicism; no disaster could perturb his hard exterior. His deeply engrained ironic attitude would let nothing affect him outwardly. So when "nothing"—and there is no immediate cause for his

The decisive action of *Tokyo Story*: Setsuko Hara bursts into tears. "Nothing, apparently, has prepared for the emotional depth of the last scene, yet it is a perfectly natural climax towards which the whole film has been moving."

weeping—does so radically effect him, it is a decisive action. It is the final disparity in an environment which had been becoming more and more disparate. It demands commitment. If a viewer accepts that scene—if he finds it credible and meaningful—he accepts a good deal more. He accepts a philosophical construct which permits total disparity—deep, illogical, suprahuman feeling with a cold, unfeeling environment. In effect, he accepts a construct such as this: there exists a deep ground of compassion and awareness which man and nature can touch intermittently. This, of course, is the Transcendent.

But, as Milne realized, "something" did prepare the viewer for the final scene of *An Autumn Afternoon*, or else he would have rejected it outright. That "something" was the transcendental style which throughout the film was constructing a form—first in the everyday, then in the progressive degrees of disparity—which could assimilate a decisive action, make it credible, and transform it into stasis.

3. *Stasis: a frozen view of life which does not resolve the disparity but transcends it.*

Stasis is the end product of transcendental style, a quiescent view of life in which the mountain is again a mountain. Step three may confront the ineffable, but its techniques are no more "mysterious" than steps one and two. There is a definite before and after, a period of disparity and a period of stasis, and between them a final moment of disparity, decisive action, which triggers the expression of the Transcendent. The transcendental style itself is neither ineffable nor magical: every effect has a cause, and if the viewer experiences stasis it is with good reason.

The decisive action does not resolve disparity, but freezes it into stasis. To the transcending mind, man and nature may be perpetually locked in conflict, but they are paradoxically one and the same. In Ozu, as in Zen, stasis evokes the moods of the *furyu* and particularly *mono no aware*. Man is again one with nature, although not without sadness. "In this respect Nature is divine. Its 'irrationality' transcends human doubts or ambiguities, and in our submitting to it, or rather accepting it, we transcend ourselves."[47]

Complete stasis, or frozen motion, is the trademark of religious art in every culture. It establishes an image of a second reality which can stand beside the ordinary reality; it represents the Wholly Other. In Ozu, the image of stasis is represented by the final coda, a still-life view which connotes Oneness. It is the same restrictive view which began the film: the mountain has become a mountain again, but in an entirely different way. Perhaps the finest image of stasis in Ozu's films is the lengthy shot of the vase in a darkened room near the end of *Late Spring*. The father and daughter are preparing to spend their last night under the same roof; she will soon be married. They calmly talk about what a nice day they had, as if it were any other day. The room is dark; the daughter asks a question of the father, but gets no answer. There is a shot of the father asleep, a shot of the daughter looking at him, a shot of the vase in the alcove and over it the sound of the father snoring. Then there is a shot of the daughter half-smiling, then a lengthy, ten-second shot of the vase again, and a return to the daughter now almost in tears, and a final return to the vase. The vase is stasis, a form which can accept

The final five shots of *Late Autumn*: "Stasis presents the same restricted view which began the film: the mountain has become a mountain again, but in an entirely different way."

deep, contradictory emotion and transform it into an expression
of something unified, permanent, transcendent.

The decisive action—the miracle of the tears—has little
meaning in itself but serves to prove the strength of the form. The
transcendental style, like the vase, is a form which expresses
something deeper than itself, the inner unity of all things. This is
a difficult but absolutely crucial point; transcendental style is a
form, not an experience. The purpose of transcendental style is
not to get the viewer to share Hirayama's tears, but to purge those
tears and integrate them into a larger form. This form, like the
mass, can encompass many emotions, but it is expressive of
something greater than those emotions. (I don't mean to drift into
ineffability here, because I believe that this "purging of tears" is
caused by solid, phenomenological reasons, but, again, I prefer to
hold off that discussion until I can write from the wider
perspective of Bresson's films.)

The everyday and disparity are experiential, however;
they taunt and tease the spectator's emotions. But stasis is
formalistic; it incorporates those emotions into a larger form. The
everyday and disparity present an obstacle course for the
emotions: they undermine the viewer's customarily rock-solid
faith in his feelings, hopefully bringing him to the point where
he is willing to accept and appreciate an idea of life in which all
emotions, however contradictory, have no power in themselves
but are only part of a universal form which expresses the inner
unity of every phenomenon. Stasis, by showing a static, quiescent,
organized scene, reinforces this newfound idea of life. If
successful, stasis transforms empathy into aesthetic appreciation,
experience into expression, emotions into form.

This distinction between form and experience is not
pedantic, but fundamental: a form can express the Transcendent,
an experience cannot. A form can express the common ground in
which all things share. An experience can only express one man's
reaction to that common ground. Both form and experience can
lead to experience, however. This conundrum perhaps can be
clarified by this sequence of possible events: a certain form (the
mass, transcendental style) expresses the Transcendent. A viewer,
perceiving and appreciating that form, undergoes the experience
of transcendence. He then seeks to evoke that same feeling in his

friend. He tells his friend exactly how he felt; his friend is curious and faintly amused, but does not share the speaker's transcendent feelings. In order to successfully induce transcendence in his friend, the viewer would have had to transform his feelings into a form (as transcendental style does) in which his friend could perceive the Transcendent, and then experience transcendence. Therefore, it is possible in *An Autumn Afternoon* for Hirayama to experience transcendence on screen, and for the viewer in the theater to experience transcendence watching him, and both not be communicating any emotion, but only a simultaneous participation in a larger form.

Decisive actions and final stasis shots are not exclusive to transcendental style. Christ's healing of the disfigured man in Pasolini's *The Gospel According to St. Matthew* and Simon's restoration of the peasant's amputated hand in Buñuel's *Simon of the Desert* are decisive actions very similar to the raising of the dead in *Ordet*, or Hirayama's tears in *An Autumn Afternoon*. Similarly, the concluding shots of Mizoguchi's *Sansho the Bailiff*, *Ugetsu Monogatari*, and Antonioni's *L'Eclisse* correspond to the final stasis shots of Ozu and Bresson: a long pull-back from the central characters, a still view of natural surroundings, and the strong implication of the unity of all existence. But the transcendental style is not defined by any one of its elements, the techniques of decisive action and stasis can exist in any film. The use of stasis does not make Antonioni a transcendental artist any more than the use of the everyday by Warhol, mild disparity by Forman, or decisive action by Buñuel make them transcendental artists. They utilize parts of the transcendental style and profit by it, but they are not exclusively concerned with the Transcendent.

An Eliade-Wolfflin–inspired analysis of transcendental style in Ozu's films may seem very similar to a cultural analysis, primarily because Zen culture incorporates the idea of transcendence. But this method, which seeks to delineate universal forms of spiritual expression, does have certain advantages when confronting similar phenomena in different cultures, such as in the case of "frontality."

Tadao Sato, in his cultural analysis, points out that Ozu's characters often directly face into the camera. Even if a character were staring at a wall one foot away, Ozu would figuratively "remove" the wall in order to shoot the actor head-on. Sato attributes this to Ozu's traditional sense of decorum and courtesy: "the camera of Yasujiro Ozu behaves toward the characters with the attitude of the host toward the guests. Conversely, the characters of Ozu's films behave themselves as if they were guests of the host."[48]

Considered as an aspect of transcendental style (first in everyday, then in stasis), however, frontality has obvious affinities with religious art in many cultures. Hieratic frontality is the characteristic of Byzantine iconography as well as primitive West African sculpture. Although Ozu used frontality to convey the gentility of traditional Japan, he more importantly used frontality the way religious artists have always used frontality: to inspire an I-Thou devotional attitude between the viewer and the work of art. The Wolfflin analysis seeks to define the roots and origins of form, and is therefore appropriate to transcendental style, which seeks to locate the roots of spiritual feeling.

Transcendental Style East and West

One can only extract so much from culture—most characteristics of a work of art are inseparably linked to their culture. Transcendental style is a "way of liberation" from the terrestrial to the Other world, and consequently its origins are necessarily intrinsic to the particular culture from which it springs. Until "liberation," the influence of culture is pervasive.

Each artist must use the raw materials of his personality and culture. Yasujiro Ozu, in particular, seems totally bound by his culture. The Japanese make little attempt to separate Ozu from his culture; they by and large consider his films only as "entertainments." And with good reason—the point at which Zen style stops and transcendental style begins is almost indiscernible in Ozu's films. It is not possible to extrapolate the transcendental style from within a totally Japanese perspective; one needs several cultural perspectives. By demonstrating how the three steps of transcendental style function in the West (in Bresson's films), it is possible not only to separate the transcendental style from Zen culture, but also to show the unity of the style. The differences between Ozu and Bresson are personal and cultural, their similarities are stylistic, but until the moment of transcendental stasis, the personal and cultural differences are all-important. If stasis is not achieved there can be no proper use

of the Eliade-Wolfflin method. Without stasis, there is no
expression of the Transcendent, and without expression of the
Transcendent, there can be no fundamental interrelation between
cultures, and without interrelation there can be no "universal
form of representation."

Although Ozu and Bresson are the exemplary directors of
transcendental style, although they both employ an everyday-
disparity-stasis progression, their films are not identical but as
different as the East from the West. The trappings of the
Transcendent, prior to stasis, are different East and West, and
Ozu and Bresson reflect these differences.

Christopher Dawson distinguishes between the cultural
trappings of the Transcendent East and West:

> Western philosophy started with the Hellenic conception
> of Nature. Its raison d'être was to explain and rationalize
> nature, and God was ultimately brought in as the
> key-stone of the philosophic edifice—as the First Cause
> or the Prime Mover. Eastern philosophy, on the other
> hand, started with the principle of Transcendent Being
> and then attempted to explain the world, or the existence
> of relative conditional existences, in terms of the
> absolute.[49]

Rudolf Otto divided these two varieties of transcendental
expression into "The Way of Unifying Vision" and "The Way
of Introspection."[50] The West tended to conceive of nature as an
opponent, or, at best, a reluctant partner who had to be subdued,
overcome and forcibly unified with man, most often through
symbolic acts. The introspective way of the East sought nature
within man, thus eliminating the classic dichotomies of Western
thought: man versus nature, body versus soul. The East sought
the Transcendent within the world, the West apart from it. But
whenever there is an expression of the Transcendent (and an
accompanying transcendental experience), whether in Śankara or
Eckhart, these differences are totally obscured: The Way of
Unifying Vision leads to introspection and the Way of
Introspection leads to Unifying Vision. This fusion is the
necessary condition of mysticism; it engenders a common
transcendental style in the East as well as the West, in film as
well as all the arts.

The difference between transcendental expression East
and West is the difference between *satori* and conversion:
"*Satori* (enlightenment) is knowing the world as it really is; not,
as some Christians believe conversion to be, something descending
from on high that changes the world."[51] *Satori* is a single flash of
awareness, but conversion is dipartite: it includes crucifixion and
resurrection, a bloody forsaking of the ego and body, and an
incorporeal entrance into glory. "Crucifixion has no meaning
whatsoever unless it is followed by resurrection," Suzuki writes.
"It is different with enlightenment (*satori*), for it instantly
transforms the earth itself into a Pure Land."[52] The difference
between transcendental expression East and West affects the
filmic transcendental style through its disparity.

The disparity in Ozu's films is primarily internal: man
cannot find nature within himself. The disparity in Bresson's films
is primarily external: man cannot live harmoniously with his
hostile environment. In Ozu, there are no futile protests against
the frailty of the body and the hostility of the environment, as in
Bresson. In Bresson, there is no resigned acceptance of
environment, as in Ozu.

The decisive action in Ozu's films is a communal event
between the members of a family or neighborhood. The decisive
action in Bresson's films is limited to a lonely figure pitted against
a hostile environment. Bresson stands in the Judeo-Christian
tradition of the single redeemer: Moses, Christ, the priests, saints,
and mystics who each in his own life righted man with the world.
Ozu does not structure his films around a specific Christ or a
specific Calvary. In Ozu's films a number of characters can
participate in the Transcendent through a number of decisive
actions.

The differences between Ozu and Bresson are unified in
stasis, the culmination of transcendental style. The Wholly
Other, once perceived, cannot be limited by culture.

II. Bresson

Robert Bresson directing *The Trial of Joan of Arc.*

The films of Robert Bresson exemplify the transcendental style in the West, but, unlike Ozu's, are estranged from their culture and are financially unsuccessful. In a medium which has been primarily intuitive, individualized and humanistic, Bresson's work is anachronistically nonintuitive, impersonal, and iconographic.

The transcendental style in Bresson's films has not been unchronicled. Amédée Ayfre, André Bazin, and Susan Sontag have all written perceptive analyses of Bresson's "Jansenist direction," "phenomenology of salvation and grace," and his "spiritual style." The qualities of transcendental style have also been chronicled by Bresson himself. Bresson is a rarity among film-makers: he apparently knows exactly what he does and why he does it. The many statements Bresson has made in interviews and discussions, properly arranged, would constitute an accurate analysis of his films (a statement which can be made of no other film-maker to my knowledge), and any study of Bresson must take into account his astute self-criticism.

Bresson's output has been meager: nine films in twenty-seven years. Bresson's career, like Ozu's, has been one of refinement, but, unlike Ozu, he served no lengthy apprenticeship. His first film, *Les Affaires Publiques* (1934), has apparently been "lost," but his second, *Les Anges du Péché* (1943), displayed what one critic called a "vision almost mature."[1] After *Les Dames du Bois de Boulogne* (1944), a film which found Bresson somewhat at odds with his material, Bresson entered into a cycle of films which present the transcendental style at its purest. The four films of the prison cycle deal with the questions of freedom and imprisonment, or, in theological terms, of free will and predestination. "All of Bresson's films have a common theme: the meaning of confinement and liberty," Susan Sontag writes. "The imagery of the religious vocation and of crime are used jointly.

Both lead to 'the cell.' "[2] All of Bresson's prison cycle films concern spiritual release: in *Diary of a Country Priest* (*Le Journal d'un Curé de Compagne*, 1950) this release occurs within the confines of a religious order, in *A Man Escaped* (*Un Condamné à Mort S'est Echappé*, 1956) it concurs with escape from prison, in *Pickpocket* (*Pickpocket*, 1959) it concurs with imprisonment, in *The Trial of Joan of Arc* (*Le Procès de Jeanne d'Arc*, 1961), it occurs both within the confines of religious belief and a physical prison. Bresson's latest three films—*Au Hasard, Balthazar* (1966), *Mouchette* (1966), and *Une Femme Douce* (1969)—have explored and expanded some of his traditional themes, but do not as yet seem (it may be too early to tell) to have achieved the resolution of the prison cycle.

Bresson's prison cycle provides an excellent opportunity to study the transcendental style in depth for several reasons: one, because the prison metaphor is endemic to certain theological questions; two, because Bresson's statements clear up much of the ambiguity in which critics are often forced to operate; and three, because there are few cultural elements intermingled with transcendental style in his films. In Ozu's films the transcendental style had to be extricated from the culture; in Bresson's films this has already happened to a large degree: Bresson is alienated from his contemporary culture.

Like Ozu, Bresson is a formalist: "A film is not a spectacle, it is in the first place a style."[3] Bresson has a rigid, predictable style which varies little from film to film, subject to subject. The content has little effect on his form. Bresson applies the same ascetic style to such "appropriate" subjects as the suffering priest in *Diary of a Country Priest* as he does to such "inappropriate" subjects as the ballroom sequences in *Les Dames du Bois de Boulogne* and the love-making sequence in *Une Femme Douce*. In discussing how accidents on the set can affect a director's style, Raymond Durgnat remarked, "It's no exaggeration to say that such stylists as Dreyer and Bresson would imperturbably maintain their characteristic styles if the entire cast suddenly turned up in pimples and wooden legs."[4]

Spiritual sentiments have often led to formalism. The liturgy, mass, hymns, hagiolatry, prayers, and incantations are all formalistic methods designed to express the Transcendent. Form, as was stated earlier, has the unique ability to express the

Transcendent repeatedly for large and varied numbers of people. Bresson's statement on his art is also applicable to religious forms and rituals: "The subject of a film is only a pretext. Form much more than content touches a viewer and elevates him."[5]

Susan Sontag has gone so far as to say that Bresson's form "*is* what he wants to say,"[6] a statement which is somewhat ambiguous because when a work of art is successful the content is indiscernible from the form. It would be more helpful to say that in Bresson's films (and in transcendental style) the form is the *operative* element—it "does the work." The subject matter becomes the vehicle (the "pretext") through which the form operates. The subject matter is not negligible; Bresson has chosen his subjects very carefully, as the term "prison cycle" indicates. But in transcendental style the form *must* be the operative element, and for a very simple reason: form is the universal element whereas the subject matter is necessarily parochial, having been determined by the particular culture from which it springs. And if a work of art is to be truly transcendent (above *any* culture), it must rely on its universal elements. Appropriately, Bresson has set his priorities straight: "I am more occupied with the special language of the cinema than with the subject of my films."[7]

Both Ozu and Bresson are formalists in the traditional religious manner; they use form as the primary method of inducing belief. This makes the viewer an active participant in the creative process—he must react contextually to the form. Religious formalism demands a precise knowledge of audience psychology; the film-maker must know, shot for shot, how the spectator will react. "I attach enormous importance to form. Enormous. And I believe that the form leads to the rhythm. Now the rhythms are all powerful. Access to the audience is before everything else a matter of rhythm."[8]

THE TRANSCENDENTAL STYLE: THE EVERYDAY

The everyday in films has precedents in religious art; it is what one Byzantine scholar calls "surface-aesthetics."[9] A fanatical attention to minute detail is evident in Chinese porcelain, Islam carpets, and Byzantine architecture (*belopoeika* and *thaumatopoike*). In the third-century Alexandrian School the study of Scripture became a matter of minute detail; the

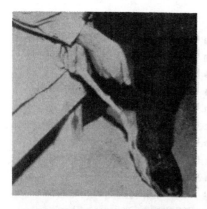
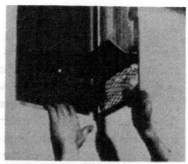

The everyday in *A Man Escaped*: "The supernatural in film is only the real rendered more precise," Bresson says. "Real things seen close up."

Alexandrine exegetes believed that mystic meanings could only be reached through concentration on each detail of the text.

In film, "surface-aesthetics" is the everyday, and is practiced by Bresson: "There is a nice quote from Leonardo da Vinci which goes something like this: 'Think about the surface of the work. Above all think about the surface.' "[10] Cinematic attention to the surface creates a documentary or quasi-documentary approach. Concerning *A Man Escaped*, Bresson told a reporter: "I really wish that it would almost be a documentary. I have kept a tone bordering upon the documentary in order to conserve this aspect of truth all the time."[11] A screen title to *A Man Escaped* reads: "This story actually happened. I set it down without embellishments." Similarly a title at the beginning of *The Trial of Joan of Arc* reads, "These are the authentic texts." Like the Alexandrine exegetes Bresson believes, "The supernatural in film is only the real rendered more precise. Real things seen close up."[12]

By taking all fact as reality, each fact with neither significance or connotation, Bresson creates a surface of reality. The "surface" is achieved, writes Ayfre, through "a very precise choice of details, objects and accessories; through gestures charged with an extremely solid reality."[13] Bresson's "reality" is a celebration of the trivial: small sounds, a door creaking, a bird chirping, a wheel turning, static views, ordinary scenery, blank faces. He uses every *obvious* documentary method: actual locations—Fort Monluc in *A Man Escaped* and the Gare de Lyon in *Pickpocket*—nonactors, and "live" sound. Yet there is no desire to capture the documentary "truth" of an event (the *cinéma-vérité*), only the surface. Bresson documents the surfaces of reality.

Bresson's everyday stylization consists of elimination rather than addition or assimilation. Bresson ruthlessly strips action of its significance; he regards a scene in terms of its fewest possibilities. A seeming trivial anecdote may illustrate this: while shooting a scene in *Diary of a Country Priest* Bresson instructed an assistant to have a man without a hat walk through the background of the scene. When, a short time later, the assistant told Bresson that the bareheaded man was ready, Bresson corrected him saying that he didn't want a bareheaded man, but a man without a hat.[14] Bresson defines reality by what Aristotle called "privation," by the qualities that an objects lacks yet has potential for. Water, for example, is defined as potential steam. In Bresson's films the bareheaded man is potentially a man with a hat, and the everyday is potentially stasis. A reality defined by privation is as desolate and without significance as one defined by nihilism, but it is also predicated upon a change. To use a scriptural metaphor, a privated universe groaneth and travaileth for its potential.

Bresson admits that the everyday is a sham: "I want to and, indeed, do make myself as much of a realist as possible, using only the raw material taken from real life. But I end up with a final realism that is not simply 'realism.' "[15] The realistic surface is just that—a surface—and the raw material taken from real life is the raw material of the Transcendent.

Bresson's use of the everyday is not derived from a concern for "real life," but from an opposition to the contrived, dramatic events which pass for real life in movies. These emotional constructs—plot, acting, camerawork, editing, music—are "screens." "There are too many things that interpose themselves. There are screens."[16] Screens prevent the viewer from seeing through the surface reality to the supernatural; they suppose that the external reality is self-sufficient.

This is why Bresson's work seems so perverse to the uninitiated viewer: Bresson despises what the moviegoer likes best. His films are "cold" and "dull"; they lack the vicarious excitement usually associated with the movies. Bresson, Sontag writes, "is pledged to ward off the easy pleasures of physical beauty and artifice for a pleasure which is more permanent, more edifying, more sincere"[17]—and the average moviegoer is unlikely to relinquish these "easy pleasures" easily. What are the "screens" and "easy pleasures" and how does Bresson ward them off?

Plot.

Like Ozu, Bresson has an antipathy toward plot: "I try more and more in my films to suppress what people call plot. Plot is a novelist's trick."[18] The plot "screen" establishes a simple, facile relationship between the viewer and event: when a spectator empathizes with an action (the hero is in danger), he can later feel smug in its resolution (the hero is saved). The viewer feels that he himself has a direct contact with the workings of life, and that it is in some manner under his control. The viewer may not know how the plot will turn out (whether the hero will be saved or not), but he knows that whatever happens the plot resolution will be a direct reaction to his feelings.

In Bresson's films the viewer's feelings have no effect on the outcome. *A Man Escaped* would seem of all Bresson's films the most plot-oriented; it is about a prison break. But the title dispenses with any possibility of suspense—*Un Condamné à Mort S'est Echappé* (a man condemned to death has escaped). In *The Trial of Joan of Arc* the viewer, of course, knows the ending, but in case of any doubt the English guard repeatedly reiterates the fact: "She will die." "She must burn." The events are predestined, beyond the viewer's control and beyond—seemingly—Bresson's.

By using plot to evoke audience empathy, a dramatist

limits the ways in which he can manipulate his audience. Even if he toys with the plot, confusing the viewer's emotions, he nonetheless restricts the result to the emotional level. "As far as I can I eliminate anything which may distract from the interior drama. For me, the cinema is an exploration within. Within the mind, the camera can do anything."[19] The internal drama is in the mind, Bresson seems to say, and emotional involvement with an external plot "distracts" from it. (There is emotional involvement with Bresson's films, but it is the emotional involvement which follows recognition of form.)

Bresson's films, of course, are not entirely devoid of "plot"; each has a succession of events which have a rise and fall, a tension and relaxation, however slight. By the term "drama," however, Bresson does not mean simply the manipulation of events, but the appeal to the emotions through the manipulation of events. This sort of drama is something imposed on films; it is not endemic to the cinematic form: "Dramatic stories should be thrown out. They have nothing whatsoever to do with cinema. It seems to me that when one tries to do something dramatic with film, one is like a man who tries to hammer with a saw. Film would have been marvelous if there hadn't been dramatic art to get in the way."[20]

Acting.

Bresson's most vehement denunciations are reserved for acting: "It is for theater, a bastard art."[21] The acting process is one of simplification; the actor modifies his personal, unfathomable complexities into relatively simple, demonstrable characteristics. "An actor, even (and above all) a talented actor gives us too simple an image of a human being, and therefore a false image."[22] "We are complex. And what the actor projects is not complex."[23]

An actor is primarily concerned with the character of the man he portrays. Bresson is concerned with how he can use that actor to convey a reality which is not limited to any one character. The actor's most convenient approach to a character is psychology, and Bresson despises psychology: "I do not like psychology and I try to avoid it."[24] Psychological acting humanizes the spiritual, "good" psychological acting even more so than "poor" psychological acting. Bresson, Bazin pointed out, is "concerned not with the psychology but with the physiology of existence."[25]

Psychological acting is the easiest and most appealing of all the screens, and therefore Bresson must work the hardest to avoid it. If not properly restrained an actor will exert a creative force in a film—and in a Bresson film, Bresson is the only one who does the creating. "You cannot be inside an actor. It is he who creates, it is not you."[26]

In order to reduce acting to physiology, Bresson carefully instructs his actors in nonexpressiveness. He forces the actor to sublimate his personality, to act in an automatic manner: "It is not so much a question of doing 'nothing' as some people have said. It is rather a question of performing without being aware of oneself, of not controlling oneself. Experience has proved to me that when I was the most 'automatic' in my work, I was the most moving."[27]

Bresson's treatment of actors is remarkably similar to Ozu's, and for the same reasons.* Both strove to eliminate any expression from the actor's performance. Neither would give the actor "hints" or explain the emotions that the actor should convey, but would give only precise, physical instructions: at what angle to hold the head, when and how far to turn the wrist, and so forth. Both used repeated rehearsals to "wear down" any ingrained or intractable self-expression, gradually transforming fresh movement into rote action, expressive intonation into bland monotone. Bresson's instructions to Roland Monod, the pastor in *A Man Escaped*, explain both the method and rationale behind this theory of acting: "Forget about tone and meaning. Don't think about what you're saying; just speak the words automatically. When someone talks, he isn't thinking about the words he uses, or even about what he wants to say. Only concerned with what he is saying, he just lets the words come out,

* Compare, for example, Ozu's statement about *Late Autumn* with Bresson's statements about drama and acting. "It's very easy," Ozu said, "to show emotion in drama: the actors cry or laugh and this conveys sad or happy feelings to the audience. But this is mere explanation. Can we really portray a man's personality and dignity by appealing to emotions? I want to make people feel what life is like without delineating dramatic ups and downs" (*Cinema*, "Ozu on Ozu: The Talkies," VI–I, p. 5).

simply and directly. When you are reading, your eye just strings together black words on white paper, set out quite neutrally on the page. It's only *after* you have read the words that you begin to dress up the simple sense of the phrases with intonation and meaning—that you interpret them. The film actor should content himself with *saying* his lines. He should not allow himself to show that he already understands them. Play nothing, explain nothing. A text should be spoken as Dinu Lipatti plays Bach. His wonderful technique simply releases the notes; understanding and emotion come later."[28]

Camerawork.

A tracking shot is a moral judgment, Jean-Luc Godard once remarked, and so, for that matter, is any camera shot. Any possible shot—high angle, close-up, pan—conveys a certain attitude toward a character, a "screen" which simplifies and interprets the character. Camera angles and pictorial composition, like music, are extremely insidious screens; they can undermine a scene without the viewer's being aware of it. A slow zoom-out or a vertical composition can substantially alter the meaning of the action within a scene.

Bresson strips the camera of its editorial powers by limiting it to one angle, one basic composition. "I change camera angles rarely. A person is not the same person if he is seen from an angle which varies greatly from the others."[29] Like Ozu, Bresson shoots his scenes from one unvarying height; unlike Ozu, who prefers the seated *tatami* position, Bresson places the camera at the chest level of a standing person. As in Ozu's films, the composition is primarily frontal with at least one character facing the camera, seeming caught between the audience and his environment. Again and again, the static, well-composed environment acts as a frame for the action: a character enters the frame, performs an action, and exits.

Bresson's static camerawork nullifies the camera's editorial prerogatives. When each action is handled in essentially the same nonexpressive manner, the viewer no longer looks to the angle and composition for "clues" to the action. Like all of Bresson's everyday techniques, his camerawork postpones emotional involvement; at this stage the viewer "accepts" Bresson's static compositions, yet is unable to understand their full purpose.

Similarly, Bresson avoids the self-serving "beautiful" image. "Painting taught me to make not beautiful images but necessary ones."[30] The beautiful image, whether attractive like *Elvira Madigan,* or gross like *Fellini Satryicon,* draws attention to itself and away from the inner drama. The beautiful image can be a screen between the spectator and the event—the pictorial images of *Adalen 31* tell the viewer more about Widenberg's idea of revolution than all his rhetoric. Bresson, on the other hand, "flattens" his images: "If you take a steam iron to your image, flattening it out, suppressing all expression by mimetism and gestures, and you put that image next to an image of the same kind, all of a sudden that image may have a violent effect on another one and both take on another appearance."[31] André Bazin pointed out that the pictorial sumptuousness of Bernanos' *Diary of a Country Priest*—the rabbit hunts, the misty air—is most vividly conveyed in Renoir's films.[32] Bresson, in his adaption of Bernanos' novel, rejected the obvious interpretation, emphasizing instead the cold factuality of the priest's environment.

Editing.

Bresson's films are edited for neither emotional climax nor editorial information. Climax cutting, whether in service of a plot or self-sufficient, elicits the artificial sort of emotional involvement which Bresson studiously avoids; metaphorical editing, whether subtle or obvious, is an editorial rather than an emotional screen, a totally artificial argument imposed from without by the film-maker. Both "interpret" the action of screen.

Like Ozu, Bresson prefers the regular, unostentatious cut. He once described *A Man Escaped* as "one long sequence" in which each shot, each event, led only to the next.[33] Bresson's editing does not pose any artificial comparisons; each shot reflects only its own surface. "The form in Bresson's films," Miss Sontag writes, "is anti-dramatic, though strongly linear. Scenes are cut short, set end to end without obvious emphasis. This method of constructing the story is most rigorously observed in *The Trial of Joan of Arc.* The film is composed of static, medium shots of people talking; the scenes are the inexorable sequence of Joan's interrogations. The principle of eliding anecdotal material is here carried to its extreme. There are no interludes of any sort. It is a very deadpan construction which puts a sharp brake on emotional involvement."[34]

The Soundtrack.

Music and sound effects are the film-maker's most subtle tools—the viewer is seldom aware of the extent to which his feelings are being manipulated by the soundtrack. The soft beat of drums or the blare of Mexicali trumpets give the spectator a textbook of information. "The ear is more creative than the eye. If I can replace a set by a sound I prefer the sound. This gives freedom to the imagination of the public. This phenomenon helps you suggest things rather than having to show them."[35]

In the everyday Bresson uses contrapuntal sound not for editorializing, but to reinforce the cold reality. The sound track consists primarily of natural sounds: wheels creaking, birds chirping, wind howling. These minute sounds can create a sense of everyday life that the camera cannot. These "close-up" sounds are like the close-up shots of Michel's hands in *Pickpocket*: they establish a great concern for the minutiae of life. And because the ear is more creative than the eye, they create this concern best when the camera is at a distance from its subject.

Bresson, keenly aware of the emotional and editorial potential of music, does not use it at all in the everyday, but instead restricts himself to common, "documentary" sounds. Almost any music artificially induced into the everyday would be a screen; every piece of music carries with it certain emotional/ editorial intonations which would interpret the scene. (Bresson, however, does use music as Ozu does, in the decisive action and in stasis. When Bresson uses music as decisive action, like the use of Mozart's Mass in C Minor in *A Man Escaped*, it is not editorializing but like Ozu's coda music is a blast of emotional music within a cold context.)

In the everyday Bresson replaces the "screens" with a form. By drawing attention to itself, the everyday stylization annuls the viewer's natural desire to participate vicariously in the action on screen. Everyday is not a case of making a viewer see life in a certain way, but rather preventing him from seeing it as he is accustomed to. The viewer desires to be "distracted" (in Bresson's terms), and will go to great lengths to find a screen which will allow him to interpret the action in a conventional manner. The viewer does not want to confront the Wholly Other or a form which expresses it.

The everyday blocks the emotional and intellectual exits, preparing the viewer for the moment when he must face the Unknown. The intractable form of the everyday will not allow the viewer to apply his natural interpretive devices. The viewer becomes aware that his feelings are being spurned; he is not called upon, as in most films, to make either intellectual or emotional judgments on what he sees. His feelings have neither place nor purpose in the schema of the everyday. "The effect of the spectator being aware of the form is to elongate or retard the emotions."[36]

But movie-goers love emotional constructs, they enjoy emotional involvement with artificial screens, and one can only sympathize with the viewer who storms out of *Diary of a Country Priest* for the same reason he storms out of Warhol's *Sleep*—it's just too "boring." Although the irate viewer's attitude is understandable, his perception is poor. He has mistaken the everyday for transcendental style, and has only seen a fraction of the film. The viewer who stays recognizes that there is more than the everyday, that Bresson has put a strangely suspicious quality into his day-to-day living. The viewer's emotions have been superficially rejected, but they have been simultaneously tantalized by the disparity.

THE TRANSCENDENTAL STYLE: DISPARITY

One of the dangers of the everyday is that it may become a screen in itself, a style rather than a stylization, an end rather than a means. The everyday eliminates the obvious emotional constructs but tacitly posits a rational one: that the world is predictable, ordered, cold. Disparity undermines the rational construct.

Disparity injects a "human density" into the unfeeling everyday, an unnatural density which grows and grows until, at the moment of decisive action, it reveals itself to be a spiritual density. In the initial steps of disparity Ozu and Bresson use different techniques to suggest a suspicious and emotional quality in the cold environment. Because Ozu's everyday stylization is more "polite" in the traditional Zen manner than Bresson's, Ozu can use what Sato called a "break in the geometrical balance" to create disparity. Ozu also makes more use of character ambivalence than Bresson does (possibly because of Ozu's background in light comedy), but both employ irony. Bresson, unlike Ozu, uses "doubling," an overemphasis of the everyday, to create disparity. Both, however, create disparity by giving their characters a sense of something deeper than themselves and their environment, a sense which culminates in the decisive action. All the techniques of disparity cast suspicion on everyday reality and suggest a need, although not a place, for emotion.

Bresson overemphasizes the everyday through what Miss Sontag calls "doubling." Through the use of repeated action and pleonastic dialogue Bresson "doubles" (or even "triples") the action, making a single event happen several times in different ways. For example: in *Pickpocket* Michel makes a daily entry into his diary. Bresson first shows the entry being written into the diary, then he has Michel read the entry over the soundtrack, "I sat in the lobby of one of the great banks of Paris." Then Bresson shows Michel actually going into one of the great banks of Paris and sitting in the lobby. The viewer has experienced the same event in three ways: through the printed word, the spoken word, and the visual action.

Bresson's favorite "doubling" technique is interior narration. In *Diary of a Country Priest*, *A Man Escaped*, and *Pickpocket* the main character narrates the on-screen action in a deadpan narration which is often only an audio replay of what the viewer has already witnessed. In *Diary of a Country Priest* the priest calls anxiously on the Vicar of Torcy. The housekeeper answers, obviously informing the priest that the vicar is not at home. The door closes and the priest leans dejectedly against it. When we hear the priest's voice, "I was so disappointed, I had to lean against the door." In *A Man Escaped* the order is reversed: first Fontaine narrates, "I slept so soundly the guard had to awaken me." Then the guard walks into his cell and says, "Get up."

Interior narration is customarily used to broaden the viewer's knowledge or feelings about an event. In Ophuls' *Letter from an Unknown Woman* and Lean's *Brief Encounter*, for example, the heroines recount their romantic experiences through narration. In each case the reflective and sensitive female voice is used as a counterpart to the harsh "male" world of action. The contrast between "female" and "male," sound and sight, narration and action expands the viewer's attitude toward the situation. Bresson, however, uses interior narration for the opposite reason: his narration does not give the viewer any new information or feelings, but only reiterates what he already knows. The viewer is conditioned to expect "new" information from narration; instead, he gets only a cold reinforcement of the everyday.

When the same thing starts happening two or three times concurrently the viewer knows he is beyond simple day-to-day realism and into the peculiar realism of Robert Bresson. The doubling does not double the viewer's knowledge or emotional reaction, it only doubles his perception of the event. Consequently, there is a schizoid reaction; one, there is the sense of meticulous detail which is a part of the everyday, and two, because the detail is doubled there is an emotional queasiness, a growing suspicion of the seemingly "realistic" rationale behind the everyday. If it is "realism," why is the action doubled, and if it isn't realism, why this obsession with details?

"The doublings," Sontag concludes, "both arrest and intensify the ordinary emotional sequence."[37] That statement, like many by Miss Sontag, is both astute and baffling, and the perceptive reader will immediately ask "How?" and "Why?," questions which Miss Sontag doesn't attempt to answer. The above description may partially explain Miss Sontag's perceptions. The "emotional sequence" is arrested because of the everyday stylization (the blocking of screens), it is intensified because of the disparity (the suspicion that the film-maker may not be interested in "reality" after all). The viewer's mood becomes wary, expectant.

Techniques like doubling cast suspicion on the everyday, and the next step of disparity goes farther: it tries to evoke a "sense" of something Wholly Other within the cold environment, a sense which gradually alienates the main character from his solid position within the everyday. Jean Sémolué has distinguished three levels of such alienation in *Diary of a Country Priest*: (1) sickness: the priest and his body, (2) social solitude: the priest and his parishioners, (3) sacred solitude: the priest and the world of sin.[38] The young priest is unable to relate to any of the elements in his environment; even nature, which does not figure in Sémolué's schema, seems hostile to the suffering priest as he collapses under the gray sky and tall, dark barren trees. At this level Bresson's theme would seem to fit his pseudodocumentary everyday technique: the unending conflict between man and environment is one of the cardinal themes of documentary art.

But the conflict is more complicated than it at first seems. The source of this alienation does not seem to be intrinsic to the priest (his neurosis, misanthropy, or paranoia) or to his environment (antagonistic parishioners, inclement weather), but seems to originate from a greater, external source. The priest is the frail vehicle of an overwhelming passion which in the context of *Diary of a Country Priest* is called the holy agony (*la Sainte Agonie*). Little by little, as if moving down the Way of the Cross, the priest comes to realize that he carries a special weight, a weight which he finally accepts: "It is not enough that Our Lord should have granted me the grace of letting me know today, through the words of my old teacher, that nothing, throughout eternity, can remove me from the place chosen for me from all eternity, that I was the prisoner of His Sacred Passion."

As in Ozu's films, the passion in *Diary of a Country Priest* is greater than a man can bear, more than his environment can receive. The young priest's cross of spiritual awareness gradually alienates him from his surroundings and eventually leads to his death.

The levels of alienation demonstrated by Sémolué are actually extensions of the holy agony. In fact, what seems to be a rejection by the environment is more accurately a rejection by the priest—and not because he wishes to estrange himself, but because he is the unwilling (at first) instrument of an overwhelming and self-mortifying passion.

1. Sickness. The priest's illness seems factual enough: his health slowly wanes and finally fails him because of what is eventually diagnosed as stomach cancer. But there is a complication: the more ill he becomes the more adamantly the priest refuses to take nourishment or rest. He feels himself condemned by the weight he must bear, and associates his agony with the sacrificial agony of Christ. His need for atonement drives him to self-mortification. He eats only small portions of bread

The sacred solitude of the country priest:
"What seems to be a rejection by the environment is more accurately
a rejection by the priest—and not because he wishes to estrange
himself, but because he is the unwilling instrument of an overwhelming
and self-mortifying passion."

dipped in wine, an alcoholic parody of the sacrament. He ignores the needs of the flesh, exerting himself until the moment of death. The physical pain seems to be real enough, but its source is ambiguous; is it cancer or the spiritual malady?

2. Social solitude. The priest's ministry is a failure. He is timid and inept; his parishioners are antagonistic—or so it seems. But it is uncertain whether the priest is actually unfit for the priesthood or whether his devouring passion blocks any attempt at ministry. At first the priest seems unduly paranoiac; he thinks his parishioners dislike him. Then he receives an anonymous note, "A person of good intentions advises you to request your transfer . . . ." But the premonition comes first: it is as if the priest willed to be unwanted. The country community at first had no more hostility toward him than they would have had toward any new young priest, but the priest's melancholy turns them against him. After an unsuccessful catechism class the priest enters in his diary, "But why the hostility of these little ones. What have I done to them?" His religious obsession has led him to believe that the mischievous children are against him. The priest's agony alienates the community, and it is an agony which he seems unable to control.

3. Sacred solitude. The priest is unable to cope with the world of sin, either in himself or others. The normal recourse of a Christian, prayer, is not open to him. "Never have I strived so much to pray," he writes. And later: "I have never felt with so much violence the physical revolt against prayer." He is able to bring peace to others, yet has none himself. This is the miracle of the empty hands: "How wonderful that we can give others a peace which we ourselves do not possess. Oh, the miracle of our empty hands." His holy agony allows him none of the temporal means of release which Church, society, and body provide. None of the temporal metaphors can satisfy his passion, so he progresses inexorably toward the metaphor of martyrdom.

On each level the priest's alienation originates in neither the environment nor himself, but in an overpowering, transcendental passion. The melancholy priest earnestly desires to be like his peers ("My God," he writes of the Vicar of Torcy, "How I would wish to have his health, his stability"), but an irresistible force drives him further and further away from them. If the origin of this holy agony is not natural (human or environmental), it is of necessity supernatural.

Disparity in *The Trial of Joan of Arc*: "It is a shock when Joan answers her corrupt inquisitors with sincerity, forthrightness, honest and complete disregard for her personal safety—she is not responding to her environment in a 1:1 ratio. She answers her judges as if she were instead speaking to her transcendental 'voices.' "

Bresson's protagonists, like the country priest, cannot find metaphors capable of expressing their agony. They are condemned to estrangement: nothing on earth will placate their inner passion, because their passion does not come from earth. Therefore they do not respond to their environment, but instead to that sense of the Other which seems much more immediate. Hence the disparity; the Bresson protagonist lives in an all-inclusive cold, factual environment, yet rather than adapting to that environment, he responds to something totally separate from it.

It is a shock when Joan of Arc answers her corrupt inquisitors with sincerity, forthrightness, honesty, and complete disregard for her personal safety—she is not responding to her environment in a 1:1 ratio. She answers her judges as if she were instead speaking to her mysterious, transcendental "voices." Similarly, in *A Man Escaped* Fontaine's desire to escape surpasses any normal prisoner motivation. He is nothing but an embodied Will to Escape; the viewer only sees him as a prisoner whose every breath strives to be free. Throughout the film Fontaine wears a ragged, filthy, and bloody shirt, and when he finally receives a package of new clothes, the viewer rejoices (or wants to rejoice) for him. Instead of trying the new clothes on, Fontaine immediately tears them up to make ropes. To Fontaine's mind (as defined by "privation") the package did not contain new clothes at all, but potential ropes. Another prisoner, who had the desire but not the passion to be free, would have used the old clothes as ropes. Fontaine's obsession is his definitive quality, and it is greater than the desire to be inside or outside of those prison walls. The prison at Fort Montluc is only the objective correlative for Fontaine's passion. In *Pickpocket*, Michel's pickpocketing has the same familiar obsessive quality; it is neither sociologically nor financially motivated, but instead is a Will to Pickpocket. And when Michel renounces pickpocketing for the love of Jeanne, his motivation is again ill-defined. The viewer senses that Michel's overburdening passion has been transferred to Jeanne, but still does not know its source.

In each case Bresson's protagonists respond to a special call which has no natural place in their environment. It is incredible that Joan the prisoner should act in such a manner before a panel of judges: nothing in the everyday has prepared the viewer for Joan's spiritual, self-mortifying actions. Each protagonist struggles to free himself from his everyday environment, to find a proper metaphor for his passion. This struggle leads Michel to prison, Fontaine to freedom, and the priest and Joan to martyrdom.

The viewer finds himself in a dilemma: the environment suggests documentary realism, yet the central character suggests spiritual passion. This dilemma produces an emotional strain: the viewer wants to empathize with Joan (as he would for any innocent person in agony), yet the everyday structure warns him that his feelings will be of no avail. Bresson seems acutely aware of this: "It seems to me that the emotion here, in this trial (and in this film), should come not so much from the agony and death of Joan as from the strange air that we breathe while she talks of her Voices, or the crown of the angel, just as she would talk of one of us or this glass carafe."[39] This "strange air" is the product of disparity: spiritual density within a factual world creates a sense of emotional weight within an unfeeling environment. As before, disparity suggests the need, but not the place, for emotions.*

The secret of transcendental style is that it can both prevent a runoff of superficial emotions (through everyday) and simultaneously sustain those same emotions (through disparity). The very detachment of emotion, whether in primitive art or Brecht, intensifies the potential emotional experience. ("Emotion cannot be projected without order and restraint."[40]) And emotion will out. The trigger to that emotional release occurs during the final stage of disparity, decisive action, and it serves to freeze the emotional into expression, the disparity into stasis.

Before the final stage of disparity, however, Bresson, like Ozu, derives ironic humor from his characters and their alienated surroundings. Irony, in fact, is almost unavoidable—Bresson's characters are so totally alienated from their environment. The country priest's paranoia is crucial, obsessive—and ridiculous. When Olivier, a foreign legionnaire on leave, offers the priest a ride to the railroad station on his motorbike, the priest reluctantly accepts and then feels the exhilaration of the ride. He then states to himself, with no hint of self-parody, that he has been allowed to taste the pleasures of youth only so his sacrifice will be more complete. Bresson also uses understatement as an ironic

---

* One can never be sure of audience reactions, but even Eric Rhode, in his argument against Bresson's religious phenomenology, makes the same point: "The Naturalism of Bresson's motifs puts an irresistible pressure on us to expect the usual sorts of explanation for behaviour; but Bresson often ignores motives, quite deliberately. We never learn why Fontaine is imprisoned, why the country priest is snubbed by his parishioners, why Michel is able to go abroad without a passport. These are only a few of the many motives withheld. Because of this unresolved pressure, his heroes arouse a considerable unease in me." Precisely. Rhode also realizes that "many of his paradoxes vanish once we make the often unconscious leap into thinking along his lines," but rejects what he terms the " 'hey presto' of Grace" (*Tower of Babel* [London: Weidenfeld & Nicolson, 1966], pp. 41–43).

commentary on his characters. In *A Man Escaped* Fontaine spends every possible moment hiding and disguising his means of escape. When it appears that his cell will be searched, his plan discovered, and he executed, Fontaine says in deadpan interior narration, "I dreaded the thought of a search."

Irony makes it possible for a film-maker to create disparity over a period of time. If a viewer does not want to completely accept the dilemma of disparity (and few do), he does not have to reject it outright but can take an ironic attitude—which is essentially a wait-and-see attitude. Such a viewer can look at the disparity from an ironic distance, seeing its tensions and humor, and does not have to commit himself. Like the disparity which produces it, irony is a technique designed to hold the spectator in the theater until the final decisive action—which does demand commitment.

The decisive action is an incredible event within the ban structure. The prescript rules of everyday fall away; there is a blast of music, an overt symbol, and an open call for emotion. The act demands commitment by the viewer (the central character has already committed himself), and without commitment there can be no stasis.

In *Diary of a Country Priest* the decisive action is the priest's death, when his frail body falls from the frame and the camera holds on a blatant symbol: the shadow of the cross cast on a wall. In *A Man Escaped* it is the nocturnal escape, with its concomitant and all-important acceptance of grace in the person of Jost. In *Pickpocket* it is Michel's imprisonment and his inexplicable expression of love for Jeanne. In *The Trial of Joan of Arc* it is Joan's martyrdom, when the camera holds on the symbol of the charred stake, which is preceded by the inexplicable symbols of the flying dove and three ringing bells.

Before these decisive actions there have been "decisive moments" which anticipate the final act. In these moments, Sémolué writes, the "hero realizes that he is right to desire what he desires, and from then on identifies himself more and more with his passion."[41] (The final decisive action is more audience-oriented: the viewer must then face the dilemma of the protagonist.) As in Ozu's early codas, these decisive moments are characterized by a blast of music. In *A Man Escaped* each interlude of Mozart's Mass in C Minor becomes a decisive moment. As in Ozu's codas, there is nothing on screen to properly receive such a burst of emotion-inducing music. On ten occasions Fontaine and his fellow prisoners rotely walk across the courtyard, emptying their slop buckets to the accompaniment of Mozart's Mass. "In *A Man Escaped* there was no direct relationship between image and music. But the music of Mozart gave the life in prison the value of ritual."[42] Joan's regular walk back and forth from her cell, accompanied by overloud door-latchings, creates the same sort of coda in *The Trial of Joan of Arc*, as do the lyrical sequences of pickpocketing in *Pickpocket*. Each of these moments call for an unexpected emotional involvement and prefigure the final decisive action.

    Pickpocket is the only film of the prison cycle which does not overtly discuss religious values, yet it is nonetheless a good example of the role of the decisive action within transcendental style. There is no invocation of the spiritual as in *Country Priest* and *Joan of Arc*, no debate of grace as in *A Man Escaped*, yet there is transcendental style, and the decisive action is the "miraculous" element within it. *Pickpocket* opens with the familiar everyday stylization: Michel is a pickpocket within a cold factual world. He displays no human feeling, either for his

The decisive action in *Pickpocket*: "How long it has taken me to come to you."

dying mother or for Jeanne, a family friend. He does, however, have a passion: pickpocketing. His obsession with pickpocketing goes beyond the normal interests of crime and questions of morality. In one of his discussions with the police inspector he contends that some men are above the law. "But how do they know who they are?" the inspector asks. "They ask themselves," Michel replies. Michel's passion, in the ways previously mentioned, creates a growing sense of disparity. Then, in a somewhat abrupt ending, Michel is apprehended and imprisoned. The police had been lying in wait at Longchamp for Michel for some time, and it is uncertain at the moment of his capture whether he was captured unaware or whether he willingly let himself be captured. In the final scene, Michel, who has led the "free" life of crime, is now in jail. Jeanne comes to visit him in prison and he, in a totally unexpected gesture, kisses her through the bars saying, "How long it has taken me to come to you." It is a "miraculous" event: the expression of love by an unfeeling man within an unfeeling environment, the transference of his passion from pickpocketing to Jeanne.

The decisive action forces the viewer into the confrontation with the Wholly Other he would normally avoid. He is faced with an explicably spiritual act within a cold environment, an act which now requests his participation and approval. Irony can no longer postpone his decision. It is a "miracle" which must be accepted or rejected.

The decisive action has a unique effect on the viewer, which may be hypothesized thus: the viewer's feelings have been consistently shunned throughout the film (everyday), yet he still has "strange" undefined feelings (disparity). The decisive action then demands an emotional commitment which the viewer gives instinctively, naturally (he wants to share Hirayama's tears, Michel's love). But having given that commitment, the viewer must now do one of two things: he can reject his feelings and refuse to take the film seriously, or he can accommodate his thinking to his feelings. If he chooses the latter, he will, having been given no emotional constructs by the director, have constructed his own "screen." He creates a translucent, mental screen through which he can cope with both his feelings and the film. This screen may be very simple. In the case of *Pickpocket* it could be: people such as Michel and Jeanne have spirits which have deep spiritual connections, and they need no earthly rationale for their love. In *Diary of a Country Priest* it could be: there is such a thing as the holy agony and the tormented priest was its victim. Bresson uses the viewer's own natural defenses, his protective mechanism, to cause him, of his own free will, to come to the identical decision Bresson had predetermined for him.

Bresson calls this the moment of "transformation": "There must, at a certain moment, be a transformation; if not, there is no art."[43] At the moment of transformation all the stripped, flat images, dialogue, camerawork, and sound effects unite to create a new screen, the one formed by the spectator: "I have noticed that the flatter the image is, the less it expresses, the more easily it is transformed in contact with other images . . . it is necessary for the images to have something in common, to participate in a sort of union."[44]

Music, as opposed to sound effects, is one of the vital elements of this transformation: "I use music as a means of transformation of what is on the screen."[45] Music, properly used, "can transport us into a region that is no longer simply terrestrial, but rather cosmic, I would even say divine."[46] Music, the "miraculous" event, and the overt symbol are components of the decisive action, which can effect a "transformation" in the spectator's mind.

This "transformation" does not resolve *disparity*, it accepts it. Disparity is the paradox of the spiritual existing within the physical, and it cannot be "resolved" by any earthly logic or human emotions. It must, as the decisive action makes inescapably clear, be accepted or rejected. If the viewer accepts the decisive action (and disparity), he accepts through his mental construct a view of life which can encompass both. On screen this is represented by stasis.

TRANSCENDENTAL STYLE: STASIS

Stasis is the quiescent, frozen, or hieratic scene which succeeds the decisive action and closes the film. It is a still re-view of the external world intended to suggest the oneness of all things. In *Diary of a Country Priest* it is the shadow of the cross, in *A Man Escaped* it is the long shot of the darkened street with Fontaine and Jost receding in the distance, in *Pickpocket* it is Michel's imprisoned face, in *The Trial of Joan of Arc* it is the charred stump of the stake.

Stasis: the final shot of *The Trial of Joan of Arc*.
"The charred stake in *Joan of Arc* is still a physical
entity, but it is also the spiritual expression of
Joan's martyrdom. In short, it is an icon."

This static view represents the "new" world in which the
spiritual and the physical can coexist, still in tension and
unresolved, but as part of a larger scheme in which all phenomena
are more or less expressive of a larger reality—the Transcendent.
In stasis, the viewer is able to crossinterpret between what seemed
to be contradictions: he can read deep emotion into the
inexpressive faces and cold environment, and he can read
factuality into the inexplicable spiritual actions. The charred stake
in *Joan of Arc* is still a physical entity, but it is also the spiritual
expression of Joan's martyrdom. In short it is—as we shall see—
an icon.

The term "transcendent" may seem to some an
exaggerated description of the effect of Bresson's stasis, and
although Bresson never nails down his intentions to any specific
term, it seems quite clear that the Transcendent is what he has in
mind: "In *A Man Escaped* I tried to make the audience feel these
extraordinary currents which existed in the German prisons of the

Resistance, the presence of something or someone unseen: a hand that directs all."[47] And again, "I would like in my films to be able to render perceptible to an audience a feeling of a man's soul and also the presence of something superior to man which can be called God."[48] Whether that "something superior" is called "extraordinary currents," "the invisible hand," or "God," it transcends immanent experience and may be called, if only for practical purposes, the Transcendent.

The moment the viewer creates his own screen, the moment he accepts disparity, Bresson has accomplished not only the task of the artist, but the task of the evangelist and iconographist as well. The evangelist is theoretically a man who evokes a conversion not by his own sophistry but by bringing the listener into contact with the divine. The transcendental style, neither magical nor ineffable in its techniques, hopes similarly to bring the viewer into contact with that transcendent ground of being—into stasis.

But just "how" does this come about? Why is it possible for a viewer, at one point, to "accept" disparity? These questions are very tricky and to some degree unanswerable. It has, I think, something fundamentally to do with the fact that disparity is an emotional experience (an "emotional strain"), whereas stasis is an expression of the Transcendent. It is not really possible to "accept" an emotional strain (or else it would no longer be a strain), but it is possible to accept an expression which includes tensional elements. And for this reason the above questions must be in the final account unanswerable. It is possible to postulate how the human emotions react to upsetting experience, but no one has ever given a satisfactory account of how the human psyche perceives a form of artistic expression.

How does experience turn to expression and return to experience? All the aestheticians who adhere to an expression theory of art have addressed themselves to this question in one way or another, and I have nothing unique to add to their debate. (In fact, the concept of transcendental style is more useful if seen from within the context of preexisting aesthetic systems; it can be thought of as form, symbol, or expression.) John Dewey, who studied the experience-expression-experience puzzle in depth, felt that emotions served to catalyze aesthetic expression: "In the development of an expressive act, the emotion operates like a magnet drawing to itself appropriate material: appropriate because it has an experienced emotional affinity for the state of mind already moving."[49] Emotions are vehicles through which the artist must act; he teases and trains the emotions until they are transformed into an expression "distinctively aesthetic."

This is pretty much, I think, the way transcendental style works. Through everyday and disparity it concurrently flaunts and tantalizes the emotions, placing the viewer under a growing emotional strain which culminates in the decisive action. Man's natural impulse for emotional stability abets the transcendental style in its effort to achieve stasis. The emotions are active; in a desire to comprehend the disparity they continually attempt to outflank the everyday. The decisive action is a carefully planned cul-de-sac for this emotional activity. It simultaneously appeals to the emotions and makes the viewer aware of their futility. This necessitates a conscious, aesthetic solution to an emotionally irresolvable dilemma. Once that aesthetic perception is made, transcendental style is no longer an experience but an expression. The emotions have proved unreliable and the mind somehow recognizes this. This purging of the emotions permits the aesthetic facility of the psyche to operate. And it can recognize transcendental style for what it is— a form designed to express the Transcendent. Then, after the expression is complete and the work of art has finished its task, the viewer can return to a life of experience, feeling the "new" emotions which result from aesthetic participation.

One can never fully answer "how" stasis is achieved. Critical method has pursued the ineffable as far as it can; Roger Fry's "gulf of mysticism" yawns wide open. If transcendental style really is a hierophany, if there really is a Transcendent, then the critic can never fully comprehend how it operates in art. He can recognize the Transcendent, he can study those methods which brought him to that realization, but that actual "why" of that realization is a mystery. Bresson's protagonists cannot reveal those reasons: Bresson's characters, Ayfre writes, "even in their most extreme confidences, never reveal anything but their mystery—like God himself." Bresson cannot reveal it: Afyre continues, "these are people whose ultimate secret is not only beyond the viewer, but beyond Bresson himself."[50] The final "why" of transcendental style is a mystery even to its creator:

"I wanted to show this miracle: an invisible hand over the prison, directing what happens and causing such and such a thing to succeed for one and not for another . . . the film is a mystery."[51] If successful, Bresson would probably be willing, like the traditional religious artist, to give co-credit to the divine. A spiritual artist can predict how an audience will react to a specific form, whether it be the mass or transcendental style, but at the moment of stasis, when art merges with mysticism, he can only, in Sontag's words, "be patient and as empty as possible."[52] "The audience must feel that I go toward the unknown, that I do not know what will happen when I arrive."[53]

In a successful work of art human experience is transformed into human expression, both personal and cultural; in a successful transcendental work of art the human forms of expression are transcended by a universal form of expression. The static view at the close of Ozu's and Bresson's films is a microcosm for the transcendental style itself: a frozen form which expresses the Transcendent—a movie hierophany.

PRETEXTS

Until stasis the influence of personality and culture are for Bresson, as for Ozu, pervasive. Bresson calls the subject matter a "pretext" for the form, but until the form is fully achieved in stasis, the "pretexts" weigh heavily on the viewer's mind. Form is the operative element in Bresson's films, but it operates through personality and culture and is necessarily influenced by them. Transcendental style is as much influenced by Bresson's cultural traditions as it is by Zen culture. Transcendental style is a common formalistic solution to similar problems in individual cultures, and before a viewer can appreciate the solution he must experience the problems.

The remainder of this chapter on Bresson will consider some of the "pretexts" of Bresson's work: his personality, his cultural traditions, theological, aesthetic, and artistic, and his synthesis of those traditions. It is easier for a Western viewer to recognize Bresson's use of culture than Ozu's. He may find the moods of the *furyu* indistinguishable, but he knows or easily understands the nuances of Western theology and aesthetics. In each case Ozu and Bresson utilize their parochial characteristics, reducing them to their common element: form.

Bresson and His Personality

Considered by itself Bresson's "personality" can be misleading. To some of Bresson's critics, both admirers and detractors, he is not only the consummate stylist but also the consummate oddball: morbid, hermetic, eccentric, obsessed with theological dilemmas in an age of social action. He is a cultural reactionary and an artistic revolutionary—and the secret to this paradox lies somewhere within his curious inner logic. Considered solely in terms of his personality, Bresson becomes an obsessive religious fanatic, a tortured, brooding, Romantic figure who because of religious training, prisoner-of-war experiences, or guilt obsession is forced to live out his neuroses on screen.

This confusion results because Bresson, unlike Ozu, has become alienated from his contemporary culture. His immediate culture has had virtually no influence on his work. Bresson's asceticism is certainly at odds with the movie tradition which has zealously celebrated every aspect of the physical. And his concern for spirituality, free will, predestination and grace is only an oblique comment on contemporary French society. Bresson is today what Ozu will be in the Japan of the near future, an artist alienated from his cultural environment.

But Bresson is not simply a displaced person, a suicidal neurotic, or an eccentric genius; he is also, and more importantly, a representative of a different and older culture which may not be immediately obvious to the modern viewer but is not irrelevant either. This older culture had a well-grounded theology and aesthetic which provided not only for the role of the individual artist, but also for the function of art in a universal, multicultural sphere. Seen from these traditions, Bresson is not neurotic or eccentric, but a self-conscious artist who has assigned himself a near-impossible task: to update an older aesthetic into a contemporary form.

In the light of this older culture, Bresson's "personality" is not unique or important. Both Ozu and Bresson were soldiers, but of the two only Bresson utilized his war experiences (as a prisoner) in his films, not just because he was different from Ozu, but because the prison metaphor is inherent to his theological tradition. Bresson may be a suicidal, hermetic person, but these are also characteristics of the culture he works from within.

The more a critic realizes Bresson's theological and

aesthetic underpinnings, the further he shies away from a purely psychological interpretation of Bresson's "personality." Bresson's personality, like those of his characters, becomes increasingly identified with his passion (or in Coomaraswamy's terms, his "thesis"). At the close of *Country Priest* the priest "gives up" his body, metamorphosing into the image of the cross; in a similar manner it may be said that Bresson's personality is enveloped by transcendental style. There are many precedents in religious art for such an approach; religious artists were often required to live out the virtues they portrayed. The Stoglav Council of 1551 decreed that the Russian iconographer should "be pure and decorous."[54] Fra Angelico, in his only recorded statement, wrote, "Art requires much calm and to paint the things of Christ one must live with Christ."[55] More recently Jacques Maritain stated, "Christian work would have the artist, as man, a saint."[56] If Bresson desires to create saints in art, tradition holds, he must become "saintly" himself, submitting his personality to the transcendent passion. In the context of his theological and aesthetic culture Bresson's personality has little value. Like the country priest's it is vain, neurotic, morbid. It only has value to the extent that it can transcend itself.

There is, however, another way one can speak of Bresson's personality (without, as was previously stated, resorting to a Jungian definition), and that is as his personal contribution to the culture from which he operates, his peculiar synthesis of his theological and artistic traditions. This will be considered in a later section.

The Theological Tradition: the Prison Metaphor

The prison metaphor is endemic to Western thought. Western theories, whether theological, psychological, or political, are inevitably couched in terms of freedom and restraint. On the theological level, the prison metaphor is linked to the fundamental body/soul dichotomy, a linkage which is made by the wellsprings of Western thought: both Plato and the Scriptures. Shortly before his death Socrates describes his body as the "soul's prison."[57] To St. Paul the body of sin is prison; he is a man in "captivity to the law of sin which is in my members. O wretched man that I am! Who shall deliver me from the body of this death" (Rom. 7:23–24). (In Christianity, however, there is redemption, after which the body becomes "the temple of the Holy" [I Cor. 6:19] and Paul becomes the "prisoner of the Lord" [Eph. 4:1].) The prison metaphor in Christianity is summed up by Calvin's statement that at death "the soul is freed from the prison house of the body."[58]

On one level the prison metaphor is a relatively straightforward representation of the body/soul conflict. His characters gradually relinquish their bodies, much in the same way Fontaine escapes prison step by step. The prison house of the body is the last impediment to the soul's emancipation. Joan of Arc puts her faith in Christ and Saint Michael half hoping, half expecting that they will come to her aid, "even if by a miracle." But when she realizes that the "miracle" of her escape will in fact be her martyrdom, she retracts her false confession and chooses death, stating, "I'd rather die than endure this suffering." The night before her execution she is given communion and questioned by Brother Isambart. "Do you believe that this is the body of Christ?" he asks. "Yes, and the only one who can deliver me," she replies. "Don't you have hope in the Lord?" Isambart asks a short time later, and Joan replies, "Yes, and with God's help I shall be in Paradise." Joan's deliverance becomes her death, and her escape from prison is the escape from her body.

As the body becomes identified with the prison, there is a natural tendency toward self-mortification. The country priest mortifies his body and at the moment of death surrenders himself into the hands of God. In Pickpocket the metaphor is reversed; Michel's prison is crime, his freedom is in jail. His is also a self-mortification, but it does not lead to death. Fontaine is the only one of Bresson's prison cycle protagonists who does not actively persecute himself, although his habits are rather ascetic. The freedom of his body coincides with the freedom of his soul, and this unique occurrence is the result of grace, a theme which Bresson handles in depth in A Man Escaped.

Intertwined with the abjuration of the body in Bresson's films is the vexing problem of suicide: If the body enslaves the soul, why not destroy the body and be free? St. Ambrose stated the case quite clearly: "Let us die, if we may leave, or if we be denied leave, yet let us die. God cannot be offended with this, when we use it for a remedy,"[59] and Augustine and Aquinas rushed to counter the argument. Marvin Zeman, in an essay on suicide in Bresson's films, has demonstrated that Bresson, particularly in his later films, has come to associate himself with a radical wing of Christianity (including, among others, St. Ambrose, John Donne, George Bernanos) which regards suicide as a positive good.[60]

In the prison cycle the natural suicidal extension of the prison metaphor is already evident. Both the country priest and Joan "give up" their lives (as Christ did on the cross) but do not die by their own hand. A suicide in *Country Priest* presents St. Ambrose's case, a case which grows stronger in *Au Hasard, Balthazar, Mouchette,* and *Une Femme Douce*: the countess has been contemplating suicide, but lacks the courage. The country priest in a long dark night of the soul brings her to a faith in God, whereupon she commits suicide. The implication is clear: the countess, having found salvation, was now "free" to die. Upon learning of her suicide the priest himself feels the temptation of suicide, although he has already chosen a more subtle course.

The prison metaphor gains in complexity and depth as Bresson extends it to the theological paradox of predestination and free will. The body/soul conflict is a dichotomy for Bresson: he prefers the soul to the body, even to the point of death; whereas the predestination/free will conflict is a paradox, it cannot be resolved by death but has to be accepted on faith. Predestination/free will is a complex and contradictory concept, and Bresson's prison metaphor adapts to this complexity. Predestinarianism, as taught to varying degrees by Augustine, Aquinas, Calvin, and Jansen, holds that man, having been previously chosen by God, is now able to choose God of his own free will. Man becomes "free" by "choosing" the predetermined will of God. God is Truth, the Truth makes you free, and freedom is choosing God. It's a neat jungle of logic which seems quite preposterous from the outside; yet from the inside, accepting certain theological givens, it is the natural thing to do.

Bresson's prison metaphor allows for this complexity. In his films man's "freedom" consists of being a "prisoner of the Lord" rather than a prisoner of the flesh. Joan of Arc seemingly chooses martyrdom of her own free will, yet the film also repeatedly emphasizes that her fate is predetermined. The opening shot with its reading of Joan's postmortem readmission into the

Church and such declamatory statements as "She will die" and
"Don't forget, she must burn" leave no question as to the
outcome. The only tension, as in predestinarianism, is whether or
not she will choose her predestined fate. In *Diary of a Country
Priest* the priest realizes he is a "prisoner of the holy agony" yet
his agony only comes to culmination when he escapes from that
other prison, the body. In *Pickpocket* Michel chooses freedom by
imprisonment; in *A Man Escaped* Fontaine chooses freedom by
escape: they are the opposite sides of the predestination/free will
paradox. Each finds true freedom through the acceptance of a
predestined grace, within or without bars.

Bresson's treatment of the prison metaphor justifies his
often rather voguish labeling as a "Jansenist." Once asked if
Fontaine was predestined Bresson replied, "Aren't we all."[61]
Bresson predestines his characters by foretelling the outcome of
their lives; the drama is whether or not the character (or the
viewer) will accept his predestined fate. Bresson treats his viewers
in the same way a Jansenist God treats his minions: "You must
leave the spectator free. And at the same time you must make
yourself loved by him. You must make him love the way in which
you render things. That is to say: show him things in the order
and the way that you love to see them and to feel them; make him
feel them, in presenting them to him, as you see them and feel
them yourself, and this while leaving him a great freedom, while
making him free."[62]

Bresson hopes to make the viewer so free (by leaving him
uncommitted during everyday and disparity) that the viewer will
be forced to make Bresson's predetermined decision (during the
decisive action). On the surface Bresson leaves the spectator
totally free; his transcendence, Bazin points out, "is something
each of us is free to refuse."[63] But once the viewer makes the
commitment, once he accepts the "presence of something
superior," then he surrenders his "freedom" and joins in that
jungle of predestinarian logic. Once on the inside, the arguments
leveled from the outside are of little avail.

The mysterious, conciliatory element in the
predestination/free will paradox is grace. Grace is the catalyst
for religious commitment because, as Jansen writes, "of the
nature of a good work which is such that no created thing can
achieve this effect without the aid of Grace."[64] Unlike Calvinism,

Jansenism holds that "common" grace is nonuniversal; it is a special gift and not everyone can receive it. The comings and goings of grace are unpredictable; one must know both how to recognize it and how to receive it. "In Jansenism, there is perhaps this, which is an impression that I have as well: it is that our lives are made at once of predestination—Jansenism, then—and of *hasard*, chance."[65]

The "chance" of grace is the theme of *A Man Escaped* whose subtitle, *"Le Vent Souffle Où Il Veut"* ("the wind bloweth where it listeth," from Jesus' conversation with Nicodemus, John 3:8), expresses the unpredictability of grace. In *A Man Escaped* a prisoner-priest writes out the subtitle/text for Fontaine. Fontaine reads these words to himself as his friend Orsini is being executed for an unsuccessful escape attempt (long shot of Fontaine in his cell window, "close up" of interior narration and of the firing squad's gunshots). Later Fontaine realizes that Orsini's death has made it possible for him to escape. His aging neighbor, Blanchet, says, "Orsini had to show you how." "How strange it is," Fontaine replies. Blanchet counters that it is not strange, and Fontaine replies that it is strange that Blanchet should say that. Earlier in the film Fontaine and the priest have a similar conversation when a Bible mysteriously appears in the priest's pocket. "It's a miracle," Fontaine says. "I was lucky," the priest replies. Grace is making itself manifest in Fontaine's life, and he is as yet only dimly aware of it.

The crucial manifestation of grace in *A Man Escaped* occurs when Fontaine, the night before his planned escape, is without warning given a cell-mate, a boy named Jost. Fontaine must then decide whether to kill Jost or take him along, and he chooses the latter. Only later, while in the process of escaping, does Fontaine realize that it takes two men to scale the prison wall, that without Jost his escape would have been a failure. It was Fontaine's acceptance of Jost and the *hasard* of grace which allowed him to escape, even though it had been predetermined from the beginning of the film (by the title) that he would escape.

In Bresson's films grace allows the protagonist to accept the parodox of predestination and free will, and Ayfre quotes Augustine to demonstrate Bresson's orthodoxy at this point: "the freedom of the will is not void through Grace, but is thereby established."[66] But it is not enough for grace to be present, man must choose to receive it. Man must *choose* that which has been predestined. Because Fontaine has previously willed to escape he can correctly accept the intervention of grace through Jost. Because Joan wills to believe her voices ("How did you know that it was an angel's voice?" she is asked. "Because I had the will to believe it," she replies) she can realize grace in death. At the close of *Pickpocket* Michel comes to an acceptance of grace in the person of Jeanne, and he says to her through the bars, "How long it has taken me to come to you." The culminant statement of grace is by the country priest, whose dying words are "All is grace." If one accepts transcendental style, then all is grace, because it is grace which allows the protagonist and the viewer to be both captive and free.

Given this theological backdrop, Bresson's "pretexts" must necessarily be different than Ozu's. In Bresson's films, as in Christian theology, transcendence is an escape from the prison of the body, an "escape" which makes one simultaneously "free from sin" and a "prisoner of the Lord." Consequently, the awareness of the Transcendent can only come after some degree of self-mortification, whether it be a foregoing of the "sins of the flesh" or death itself. Prison is the dominant metaphor of Bresson's films, but it is a two-faced metaphor: his characters are both escaping from a prison of one sort and surrendering to a prison of another. And the prison his protagonists ultimately escape is the most confining prison of all, the body. In a sense, Bresson "mortified" his actors; he not only killed them fictionally, but also artistically, refusing to use an actor in more than one film.* The actor had been "worn out"; in the next film there was a new (but similar) actor who had to be mortified.

In contrast, Ozu did not feel the need to compare the tension between man and nature, soul and body, to that between a prisoner and a prison. Self-mortification had little place in his films. There were no chains, bars, persecutions, self-flagellations. The "new body" was available on earth; his characters did not need to undergo the death of the old body. Ozu used a "family"

* When asked if he would use Claude Laydu, the priest in *Country Priest*, again Bresson replied, "No. How can I? For *Journal* I robbed him of what I needed to make the film. How could I rob him twice?" (quoted in Marjorie Greene, "Robert Bresson," *Film Quarterly*, XIII, No. 3 [Spring, 1960], p. 7).

The beginning of *A Man Escaped* and the end of
Pickpocket: "Imprisonment is the dominant
metaphor in Bresson's films, but it is a two-faced
metaphor: his protagonists are both escaping from a
prison of one sort and surrendering to a prison of
another."

of actors whom he did not "kill off" but put through the same tensions in film after film. For Ozu grace was neither limited nor unpredictable, but easily available to all. The awareness of the Transcendent was for Ozu a way of living, not, as for Bresson, a way of dying.

The Aesthetic Tradition: Scholasticism

Bresson's theology, his formulation of the problems of body and soul, predestination and free will, grace and redemption, seems obviously Jansenist, but to infer from this, as some critics have, that his aesthetic and artistic influences were also Jansenist is incorrect. Jansenism, like Calvinism, had little feeling for aesthetics or art in general, and almost none for the "visual arts" in particular. Certain art forms were favored by Jansenism and Calvinism (church music and architecture), and there were maverick "Calvinist" artists (Donne, Revius, Rembrandt), but neither of these sects developed a positive aesthetic or promoted any movement in art. "Images" had little place in their logical theology,* a theology which could lead, in its excesses, to iconoclasm. Jansenism could give Bresson some of its leann ss and asceticism, but it certainly would have had no symp athy for a work of art which sought to express the Transcendent in a nonsectarian manner through images— particularly if that work of art considered its religious subject matter a "pretext." Bresson, the artist, received no aid or comfort from Jansenism; he had to look elsewhere for his aesthetics.

Bresson's immediate culture was also unable to provide the aesthetics Jansenism lacked. There has been little sympathy in modern culture in general, and cinema in particular, for the spiritual problems which troubled Bresson. There has been, of course, a twentieth-century revival of interest in the relations between form and inner meaning in the contemporary arts, and Bresson has been on the forefront of this. But in cinema this has been to a substantial degree Bresson's creation, not his "tradition."

---

* "At the rationalizing stage of religion," Herbert Read points out, "when religion becomes more than anything else an affair of philosophical concepts and of individual mediation, then there is bound to grow up a feeling that religion can dispense with such materialistic representations as works of art" (*Art and Society* [New York: Schocken Books, 1966]. p. 50).

There have been, however, several traditions in Western art which correspond remarkably to both Bresson's theological problems and his artistic solutions. And although one can never be certain where Bresson got his aesthetics, some preliminary research reveals that although he is alienated, he is not *sui generis*, and his particular approach is part of a long, though presently dormant in film, artistic tradition.

Ananda Coomaraswamy writes:

> It should be remembered that 'European art' is of two very different kinds, one Christian and scholastic, the other post-Renaissance and personal. It will be evident enough from our essay on Eckhart, and might have been made equally clear through a study of St. Thomas and his sources, that there was a time when Europe and Asia could and did actually understand each other very well.[67]

The Scholastic tradition, of which Dr. Coomaraswamy writes, would have appreciated the films of Ozu and Bresson. Ozu and Bresson have little in common theologically or culturally, but they both share in the legacy of Scholasticism, the last major pre-Renaissance aesthetic.

Neither St. Thomas nor any of the Schoolmen wrote a specific treatise on aesthetics, but in *Art and Scholasticism* Jacques Maritain extrapolates a Scholastic definition of art as an "intellectual virtue,"[68] a definition which corresponds quite closely to Coomaraswamy's definition of Asian art as "a delight of the reason."[69] "Art seems to be nothing other than a certain ordination of reason," Aquinas wrote, "by which human acts reach a determined end through determined means."[70] Art for both the Scholastic theologian and Asian artist sought an idea (beauty, nature) which was both in the world and transcended it.

The Scholastic aesthetic provides a common meeting place for East and West, and by extension, for Ozu and Bresson. It was a primitive aesthetic which had become traditional, gathering to itself a rationalized organon of thought while retaining its ultimate respect for mystery. Ideal portraiture changed: the primitive totem became a disembodied idea, but it was only a change in degree. Whether totem or idea, the end of art was mystery, and not bound by any rationalized, humanized, or secularized concepts of life. All art, like all theology and scripture, are (to use Augustine's word) "vain"; they are the means to an end, but not to be confused with the end. The artist too is a means, and his end is not himself. This aesthetic leads naturally enough to an art form, which, Coomaraswamy writes, could be either abstract or anthropomorphic, but was not sentimentalized or humanized. Bresson's use of unsentimentalized form, his pursuit of "mystery" certainly seems part of this tradition, and would explain his stylistic, although not theological, affinities with Ozu.

The Scholastic aesthetic is also appropriate for Bresson's art because it allows a place for the intellectual formulation of ideas within the form. Logic was not opposed to mystery but just another means to appreciate it. The Schoolmen "attempted a task not yet clearly envisaged by their forerunners and ruefully to be abandoned by their successors, the mystics and the nominalists: the task of writing a permanent peace treaty between faith and reason."[71] This aesthetic, which could serve both faith and reason in East and West, can also serve the seemingly contradictory qualities of Bresson's film-making.

Scholasticism, Erwin Panofsky has demonstrated, found its clearest expression in Gothic architecture. The Schoolmen define Gothic architecture by its mathematical unity rather than its later expressionist facade. Like St. Thomas' *Summa Theologiae* the Gothic world sought to create clarity through organization, synthesis through form. It represented, Panofsky writes, an "acceptance and ultimate reconciliation of contradictory possibilities."[72] On this level one could draw certain obvious parallels between Gothic architecture and Bresson's films. Both enclosed theological paradoxes within a larger form, both favored the anonymity of the artist, both sought to evoke the final "mystery."

The Gothic cathedral may be an appropriate aesthetic metaphor for Bresson's films, but in artistic practice its delicate coalition between faith and reason began to break down, more and more producing not spiritual stasis but sensual disparity. Gothic architecture, which quite literally forced faith and reason to remain under the same roof, eventually cracked under its internal strain, and its previously calm rational aesthetic became exaggerated, yielding to contorted lines and distorted figures.

Artistically, Bresson's films bear more resemblance to Byzantine portraiture, an art form which lived out an aesthetic similar to Scholasticism before there was the need to create an aesthetic.

THE ARTISTIC TRADITION: BYZANTINE ICONOGRAPHY

There undoubtedly are many major and minor artistic traditions which have influenced Bresson in one way or another, but the most important, I think, is Byzantine iconography. It has been a common thread in Western and Oriental art and influenced the Scholastic aesthetic; it serves to further strengthen the link between Bresson, Ozu, and the universal form of representation.

Like Oriental art, Byzantine iconography was an art of fixed ends, and those ends were spiritual and ideal rather than human and sentimental. The work of art was the means to an ineffable end: "The adoration of the icon," St. Basil stated, "passes to the prototype, that is to say to the Holy person represented."[73]

To achieve these ends Byzantine art was anonymous and impersonal. Some icons were described as pictures "made without hands," formed, rather, by miraculous contact with the original. To enforce anonymity Late Byzantine mosaicists were enjoined by ecclesiastical fiat to make their representations of Christ conform to certain requirements. This rule, one scholar wrote, "was designed to promote, not the artistic merit of the mosaic, but the honor of Christ; and since the majesty of Christ was the transcendent idea, of which the mosaic was the material image, this rule actually helped to draw the attention of both the mosaicist and the spectator to the right quarter."[74] Individual influence was, of course, discernible, but not peremptory; artists came and went, Byzantine iconography stayed.

Byzantine iconography was a function of the liturgy. The spectator's attitude toward the icon was the same as his attitude toward the mass. The individual became absorbed into the collective order, the collective order hardened into a form, and the form expressed the Transcendent. Consequently, the icons became stylized, rigid, hierarchical, further and further apart from the world of verisimilitude and sensation. "In the Byzantine era Christian iconography had, slowly but surely, climbed away from the alluring world of the senses, soaring ever higher into a region of theological symbolism and, through its images, carrying man's imagination to the transcendent realm where images hovered between God and man."[75]

The Schoolmen were influenced, primarily through the writings of the Neoplatonists, by Byzantine iconography and its attitudes toward art. Aquinas' artistic contemporaries, the Late Byzantine and Romanesque painters, may have been aesthetically influenced by Scholasticism but they were artistically stimulated by the Byzantine techniques they saw in imported icons and in the work of refugees from the Iconoclastic controversies. Byzantine iconography has been a continuous influence on European art. Long after the decline of Byzantium, its art molded painters like Cimabue, Duccio, Cavallini, and Giotto; affected Quattrocento painters like Mantegna; and was the basis of Carolingian, Northumbrian, and Ottonian art. Byzantine art often functioned in this manner, breathing fresh Eastern life into stagnating, rationalistic Western theories. Byzantine iconography may be seen to affect Bresson's films in the way it affected European art until as late as the sixteenth century (and in some cases, such as Rouault and Derain, until the present); it brings the force of specific, hieratic, "spiritual" techniques to a rationalized organon.

Bresson uses methods of representation very similar to those employed by Byzantine painters and mosaicists, and for some of the same reasons. Barthélémy Amengual has already noted, in passing, the similarities between Bresson's films and Byzantine art. In both, he writes, there is the "dialectic of concrete and abstract . . . the proximity, almost the identity, of the sensual and the spiritual, of emotion and idea, of static body and mobile mind."[76] The analogy can be carried even further; there are technical as well as theoretical similarities between Bresson's films and Byzantine iconography.

Frontality, nonexpressive faces, hieratic postures, symmetric compositions, and two-dimensionality are common to both. The Byzantine mosaicist constructed the nonexpressive face because God himself was beyond all expression; similarly, Bresson uses the nonexpressive face to "deprejudice" the viewer's attitudes toward the Transcendent. Bresson's statement about taking a steam iron to the image, "flattening it out," could have been written by the Stoglav Council which prohibited the

"sensuality of heretics" in iconic portraiture.[77] Frontality in
iconography was designed, Agathias wrote, so that "the man
looking at the ikon directs his mind to a higher contemplation. No
longer has he a confused veneration."[78] Bresson uses frontality
to create a respectful, noncommitted attitude within the viewer
which can result in a stasis very similar to that evoked by a
religious icon.

The long forehead, the lean features, the closed lips, the
blank stare, the frontal view, the flat light, the uncluttered
background, the stationary camera, these identify Bresson's
protagonists as objects suitable for veneration. When Michel's
cold face stares into the camera in scene after scene in *Pickpocket*,
Bresson is using his face—only one part of Bresson's complex
film-making—like a Byzantine face painted high on a temple wall.
It can simultaneously evoke sense of distance (its imposing,
hieratic quality) and a strange sensuousness (the hard-chiseled
stern face amid a vast mosaic or environmental panorama). And
when Bresson brings the rest of his film-making abilities to bear
on that face, it takes its rightful place in the liturgy. Just before
the priest collapses in fatigue on a barren hillock, almost
enveloped by gray dusk and dark barren trees, there is a long shot
in Bresson's *Country Priest* which creates a composition familiar

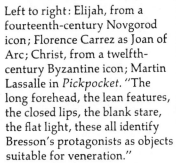

Left to right: Elijah, from a fourteenth-century Novgorod icon; Florence Carrez as Joan of Arc; Christ, from a twelfth-century Byzantine icon; Martin Lassalle in *Pickpocket*. "The long forehead, the lean features, the closed lips, the blank stare, the flat light, these all identify Bresson's protagonists as objects suitable for veneration."

to Byzantine wall paintings, such as the Ascension mosaic at St. Sophia: an agonized, lonely, full figure set against an empty environment, his head hung to the left, wrapped body-obscuring robes, about to succumb to the spiritual weight he must bear.

It is possible, but not profitable, to continue this analogy between Bresson's faces and compositions and Byzantine mosaics and paintings. One might draw comparisons to the Christ types in Byzantine portraiture, Christ the Pantokrator, Christ the King of Kings, Christ the Merciful, Christ the Suffering, and so forth, or one might compare the "three-circle" method of Byzantine painting to Bresson's lighting. But such comparisons would overextend the value of the analogy. Motion pictures are so different from mosaics that any 1:1 comparison would be inaccurate. Bresson's films are more than filmic adaptions of Byzantine icons, just as Ozu's films are more than screen versions of *sumi-e* paintings.

Ascension mosaic at St. Sophia and Claude Laydu in *Diary of a Country Priest*: "An agonized, lonely full figure set against an empty environment, his head hung to the left, wrapped in body-obscuring robes, and about to succumb to the spiritual weight he must bear."

To mold his modern-day saints Bresson draws on the
specific techniques of the long-standing tradition of Byzantine art.
These techniques not only produce certain desired, tried-and-true
audience reactions, but they also link Bresson's work to a method
of representation which has its roots in the East and has been
successfully adapted to dozens of cultures. Unlike his other
artistic traditions, Byzantine iconography ties Bresson to a
universal form which has been used by many artists, among them
Yasujiro Ozu. The common historical aesthetic and artistic
traditions shared by Bresson and Ozu, even though seemingly
remote, sets the stage for their contemporary stylistic union.

A Synthesis of Tradition: Imago Dei

Bresson is a man of (at least) three traditions. Although it
is possible to delineate each of these traditions and analyze them
separately, in the course of his films these traditions must
necessarily join and disjoin, forming more or less lasting
syntheses .The necessity of cultural syntheses was not so evident
in the study of Ozu's films because, although several
subtraditions were noticeable (such as light comedy), it seemed
(at least to this Western mind) that he, by and large, adhered to
one overriding tradition, Zen, with all its "theological," aesthetic,
and artistic implications.

One of the most interesting of Bresson's syntheses is his depiction of the Image of God. *Imago Dei* is the pivotal concept in any discussion of Christian art, and Bresson's handling of it demonstrates how he applied Byzantine concepts of portraiture to Jansenist theology. The very fact that an artist should become involved in the Image of God controversy is determined, van der Leeuw contends, by the fact that he thinks historically and transcendentally.[79] In Christianity and the West the Transcendent is fixed in a single person, the Redeemer, both God and man, and how to portray that person must be the crucial question of religious art.

Historically, there have been two interpretations of *Imago Dei*, the Eastern Orthodox and the Protestant, with the Roman church straddling the area in between. Both start from a common point: the original unity of God and man when God created man in his image (Gen. 1:26, 27). One camp, which is exemplified by the Protestant churches, takes as its text Exodus 20:3 which prohibits any graven image. The unity had been shattered by the Fall; sin-dominated man could not possibly depict the Holy. This view was expressed as early as the second century by Clement of Alexandria: "It has been plainly forbidden us to practice deceptive art; for the prophet says, 'Thou shalt not make the likeness of anything that is in Heaven, or in the earth beneath.' "[80] This notion has enjoyed continuous favor, being articulated by the eighth-century Iconoclasts, espoused to more moderate degrees by Anselm, Luther, and Calvin, and it assumed its most virulent form when Cromwell's Puritans smashed England's religious statuary. The Protestants have taken a theoretical stand against religious images of any sort (although in practice certain images have been tolerated), whereas the Roman Church continues to permit images so long as they are not worshiped or venerated.

On the other hand, the Eastern Church takes as its proof text Philippians 2:6, which emphasizes the incarnation, the fact that God came down "taking the form of a servant, being born in the likeness of a man." The Eastern view holds that as Christ is the image of God, so he can be worshiped through images. The Synod of Trullo (692) legalized this position, decreeing that "from now on icons should show . . . Christ our God in His human shape . . . so that we may be reminded of his incarnate life."[81] The Western Church saw in images (to the extent that they were permitted) only instruction, education, and edification; the Eastern Church, on the other hand, saw in images mysteries which effect salvation. The Eastern Church not only allowed images but prescribed the form they should take.

Viewed from the Roman or Protestant (which would also include the Jansenist) position Bresson engages in the heresy of Eastern iconography. The *Imago Dei* dilemma comes up in *The Trial of Joan of Arc*. The inquisitor asks Joan if her followers had made any images of her. This is a crucial question: the Roman Church is trying to convict her for the Eastern heresy of images. If Joan permits her followers to venerate images of her she is committing a double sin: blasphemy (setting herself up against God) and the creation of graven images. Joan answers with typical ambiguity, "I saw one." Bresson, with his own ambiguity, is admitting the iconographic heresy into the theology of the Western Church. Joan was not only a saint in the Roman Catholic sense (she was later canonized), that is a person whose life offers edification to those who contemplate and emulate it; but she was also, Bresson suggests, an image in the Eastern sense—an icon to be venerated. And Bresson goes on to posit an even more insidious heresy—that Joan is a spiritual icon in a Godless universe, that she should be venerated for her ability to transcend herself, thereby expressing an undefined "Transcendent" which is not any specific "God."

Bresson cannot be tied down to any one heresy; he is a heretic all his own. His techniques of portraiture come from Byzantium, his theology of predestination, free will and grace from Jansenism, his aesthetics from Scholasticism. To each tradition he brings the virtues of the other, and to cinema he brings the virtues of all three. Perhaps this is why no religious denomination has ever embraced Bresson's seemingly religious films; they haven't figured out what sort of heretic he is yet.

BEYOND PRETEXTS

From this baffling maze of traditions and subtraditions, some perhaps more or less real than I have postulated, Bresson forges what could be called *his* tradition—a curious amalgamation of Western skeletons. Yet this synthesis is only a "pretext," the cultural elements Bresson finds easiest to work with. It seems only natural for the elements of Bresson's historical traditions to coalesce for they must prepare to meet a formidable opponent: the "new," sensual, individualistic art of cinema, which with *its* traditions has tried to squash the spiritual qualities out of art. The resulting conflict pits the two traditions against each other in a bizarre time-machine manner: Scholastic aesthetic against movie aesthetic, ideal portraiture against individual portraiture, spiritual refinement against dramatic development. (The implications of the expression of the spiritual occurring on film, of course, are somewhat involved and will be considered in the Conclusion.) Out of this struggle comes a new form: transcendental style. It is the old aesthetic in the new medium. The aesthetic is familiar, but the style is new.

On the surface there would seem little to link Ozu and Bresson; neither of them could make films in the other's country without experiencing "culture shock." They shared an ancient Christian/Oriental aesthetic heritage which had fallen into general disrepair, especially in motion pictures. But their common desire to express the Transcendent on film made that link crucial; each took the old aesthetic principles into a new art form. The

Transcendence in East and West, Ozu's *Late Spring* and Bresson's *The Trial of Joan of Arc*: "For Ozu, the awareness of the transcendent was a way of living; for Bresson, a way of dying."

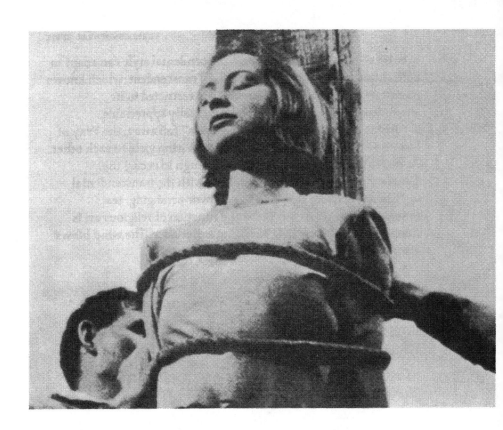

aesthetic was the same, the medium was the same, and not surprisingly, the resultant style was remarkably similar.

Transcendental style, like Byzantine art, is a universal form because it can accommodate different artists and different cultures within a common structure. Byzantine art could reach from England and France to the Far East; transcendental style can reach to wherever men make movies. The differences which seem so culturally unbridgeable can both function within transcendental style: frontality can be both Pantokrator hierarchism or it can be Zen "politeness"; disparity can be both alienation between man and nature and man and God; stasis can both be a quiescent view of nature and the symbolic icon. Transcendental style can express the endemic metaphors of each culture: it is like the mountain which is a mountain, doesn't seem to be a mountain, then is a mountain again; it is also like the prison in which man is involuntarily enclosed, yet from which through a dark night of the soul he can escape, choosing instead to enter a "new" prison. In sum, transcendental style can adapt to both cultures because it expresses the Transcendent, which knows no culture. It is not a metaphor which is restricted to its antecedents; it is a form which is universally appreciable.

At the moment of stasis the "pretexts" fall away, the Way of Introspection and the Way of Unifying Vision yield to each other. At such a moment (if it is fortunate enough to occur) the transcendental style in films is unified with the transcendental style in any art, mosaics, painting, flower-arranging, tea ceremony, liturgy. At this point the function of religious art is complete; it may now fade back into experience. The wind blows where it will; it doesn't matter once all is grace.

III. Dreyer

Carl Dreyer

This essay has sought to track down a transcendental
style—a universal form, which is used by different
film-makers in divergent cultures in order to express the Wholly
Other. This search has led to two directors who, although as
culturally alien as two men are likely to be, used similar
techniques for similar reasons. Yasujiro Ozu and Robert Bresson
seemingly have contrasting conceptions of all of man's
fundamental dilemmas: his attitudes concerning nature, death,
the body, love, grace; yet they share a common element, the need
to express that Other in form, which for them means film form.

Ayfre writes, "The style of transcendence does not allow
wavering or half-measures—to attempt it without complete
mastery is to invite disaster."* If this were so, this study of
transcendental style might well end here. Ozu and Bresson are the

---

* Ayfre continues, "A lack of rigor in style, incertainties in inspiration,
condescension and bad faith toward the audience, are enough to deprive
many works of any truly sacred meaning" (*Cinéma et la Foi Chretienne*
[Paris: Librairie Arthème Fayard, 1960], p. 87). Ayfre's definition of the
"style of transcendence" differs from the definition of transcendental style
used in this essay, not in the final result of that style ("the Invisible is
evoked rather than represented" [ibid. 85]) but in description of the
techniques which lead up to the final result. Ayfre, as far as I can tell,
defines the "style of transcendence" by its end result, its intentions, its
inner theology, its tone, but not by its specific techniques. His "definition"
is, by and large, a description of the films which evoke the desired end,
primarily the films of Bresson and Dreyer. It is not a definition of a distinct
style. He does mention certain stylistic elements in these films, "the
meticulous selection of highly concrete details," "liturgical purity," "the
Holy Face," "extreme stylization," "an undecipherable but undeniable
secret" in the character which gives the "sense that life is something
unique which does not belong to men," but he does not demonstrate, at
least to my mind, how these elements—present in many films, secular as
well as sacred—are welded into a peculiarly transcendental style. Because
Ayfre defines transcendental style by the effect evoked by its successful
examples rather than by the organization of its component parts, he falls
into the trap of mistaking partial successes for "disasters" and also, as is the
case in Dreyer's films, mistaking partial successes for complete successes.

masters of the transcendental style; they exemplify its use in
East and West. Any other film which employs transcendental
style without "complete mastery" would be, in Ayfre's terms, a
"disaster." But the case seems to be just the opposite. Any style
which is composed of definite components can be used
componentially. These components have their own identity and
function, and they can bring partial or substantial success to films
even though they are used in parody of the Transcendent (Bunuel,
Warhol), for totally secular ends (Forman, Antonioni), or in
service to a Transcendent, however vague, but without "complete
mastery" (Dreyer, Boetticher, Rosselini).

For a film-maker, the selection of the transcendental style
is not an easy one. A film-maker truly devoted to expressing the
Transcendent on film must not only eschew the more superficial
elements of his personality and culture, but he must also sacrifice
the vicarious enjoyments that cinema seems uniquely able to
provide, empathy for character, plot, and fast movement. Ozu
took many years to achieve a purified transcendental style;
Bresson arrived there much quicker, but not without considerable
introspection and determination. In the films of Carl Dreyer one
can see this struggle at work. Dreyer never totally yielded to the
transcendental style; he respected it, pioneered many of its
techniques, gradually came to use it more and more, but was
never willing to completely forsake the expressive, psychological
techniques at which he was also expert. His reluctance was not
unwitting; on the contrary, his doubts about transcendental style
stem from his fundamental doubts about the nature of the
Transcendent in life and art. Throughout Dreyer's films and his
writings about film there runs a consistent thread of ambiguity:
whether art should express the Transcendent or the person
(fictional character or film-maker) who experiences the
Transcendent; whether the Transcendent is an outer reality or an
inner reality. Toward the end of his life (he died in 1968), Dreyer
seemed to be moving more and more toward an austere,
predominantly transcendental style, but he never forsook his
fundamental spiritual—and therefore stylistic—dualism.

Like Bresson, Dreyer had a meager film output: fourteen
films in fifty-nine years. He was plagued with the financial
difficulties so familiar to Bresson. Audiences often found his films
"static" and "boring"; he lived from one critical "rediscovery" to

the next. He lived in a time and place even less receptive to the solitary, uncorruptible artist than Bresson's. During the most mature, profound period of his directorial career, from the age of thirty-nine to his death at seventy-nine, he was able to make only six features.

Unlike Ozu and Bresson, however, Dreyer was not an unwavering formalist; he did not define a single style throughout his career. On the contrary, Dreyer was proud of the fact that he had been able to create a different style for each of his films: "A Danish critic said to me one day, 'I have the impression that there are at least six of your films that are stylistically completely different, one from the other.' That moved me, for that is something I really tried to do: to find a style that has value for only a single film."[1] Dreyer did not devote his life to the rarification of the transcendental style, yet it was one of the recurring, fundamental elements in his approach to film.

Each of Dreyer's individual film "styles" is, to be more accurate, a synthesis between three basic and opposing styles at work in his films. In his study of Dreyer, Claude Perrin notes two of these opposing forces. "In order to define Dreyer's aesthetic," he writes, "one must confront two opposing artistic schools: the Kammerspiel and expressionism."[2] Perrin goes on to demonstrate how the tension between these "schools" underlies all of Dreyer's work. This tension, to be sure, is integral to Dreyer's films, but, it seems to me, it is unable to account for that peculiar, "spiritual" quality Perrin and others ascribe to his work. A "fundamental opposition" between Kammerspiel and expressionism was a consistent stylistic feature of the early German cinema, as Lotte Eisner points out;[3] yet none of the German films evoke a world of transcendent values in the way Dreyer's films do. There is, I suggest, another force—transcendental style—which interacts with both Kammerspiel and expressionism in Dreyer's films, and brings them each a certain spiritual weight which they do not innately possess. Of the three "styles," Kammerspiel is the artistic raw material of Dreyer's films; expressionism and transcendental style act upon and distort that material, turning it to their own ends. Expressionism and transcendental style are both in opposition to Kammerspiel, but they are more crucially in opposition to each other, and one usually succeeds at the expense of the other.

The interplay of these forces, styles, or schools in
Dreyer's films may be schematized thus: (1) some films are
straightforward, relatively unhampered Kammerspiel, such as
Mikael (1924), *Master of the House* (*Du Skal Aere Din Hustru*,
1925), *Two People* (*Tva Manniskor*, 1945), *Gertrud* (1965); (2)
in one film, *Vampire* (*Vampyr*, 1932), expressionism
predominates over Kammerspiel and transcendental style; (3) in
another, *The Word* (*Ordet*, 1955), transcendental style
predominates over Kammerspiel and expressionism; (4) in
others, most importantly *The Passion of Joan of Arc* (*La Passion
de Jeanne d'Arc*, 1928) and *Day of Wrath* (*Vredans Dag*, 1943),
expressionism and transcendental style vie for control of the
Kammerspiel.

KAMMERSPIELFILM

The late nineteenth- and early twentieth-century
Kammerspiele (literally, chamber plays) were the immediate
stylistic precedents for Dreyer's films; they influenced both his
choice of subject and directorial method. Kammerspiele were
a reaction against the elaborate showcase staging of classical
drama; they desired to create an "intimate theater" in which the
effect of chamber music could be transferred to the stage. Max
Reinhardt founded *Die Kammerspiele* in 1906 and August
Strindberg started his Intimate Theater the following year. In
these small theaters with dim lights and warm-toned wood
paneling, an elite (not more than three hundred spectators) could
"feel all the significance of a smile, a hesitation, or an eloquent
silence."[4] The chamber plays themselves, like those written by
Strindberg for his theater, were equally "intimate," featuring a
slow-paced drama between members of a "family" (or social
group) within a "house" (fixed number of rooms). These were the
limits—both physical and thematic—in which psychological
depths could be probed.

"In drama," Strindberg wrote his actors, "we seek the
strong, highly significant motif, but with limitations. We try to
avoid in the treatment all frivolity, all calculated effects, places
for applause, star roles, solo numbers."[5] Kammerspiele have a
simplicity of scenic means, a refusal to use declamatory effects, a
systematic realism, rigorous action, and a measured symbolism.

Kammerspiel in *Mikael*: "Complex psychological states are revealed through meticulous staging, an insinuating manner, weighty deeply felt gestures, and a ponderous slowness."

The Kammerspielfilm (the chamber play transferred to the screen), Miss Eisner writes, "is the psychological film *par excellence.*"[6] Complex psychological states were revealed through meticulous staging, an insinuating manner, weighty, deeply-felt gestures, and a ponderous slowness. In sum, Kammerspiele are distinguished from conventional drawing-room dramas by a Nordic sober-mindedness, a simplicity of artistic means, and a weighty psychological intent.

Dreyer was not only aware but proud of his origins in the "intimate" psychological Kammerspiele. He once described *Mikael* as a true Kammerspielfilm,[7] and later said he was flattered that *Mikael* had been called the first Kammerspielfilm.[8] In each of Dreyer's films one can detect elements of Kammerspiele: intimate family drama, fixed interior settings, unembellished sets, long takes emphasizing staging, the use to gesture and facial expression to convey psychological states, plain language, and a thoroughgoing sobriety. *Master of the House*, for example, contains almost all these elements; its enclosed interiors, its measured pacing, its emphasis on revelatory gesture, all place it within the Kammerspiele tradition.

Dreyer's roots in Kammerspiele are most evident in his treatment of actors. He puts great faith in his actors; he does not impress a stylization *upon* his actors, like expressionism or transcendental style, but teases expression *out* of them. "The director is careful never to force his own interpretation on an actor, because an actor cannot create truth and pure emotions on command. One cannot push feelings out. They have to arise from themselves, and it is the director's and actor's work in unison to bring them to that point."[9] Consequently Dreyer, like the director of the Intimate Theater, places great emphasis on the revelatory nuances of gesture and expression: "In French and American psychological films of recent years, facial expression is again brought to honor and given value, and it is all to the good . . . gesture endows the face with soul and facial expression is an extra-important plus to the spoken word . . . the wrinkles in a face, small as well as large, tell you endlessly about the character."[10]

EXPRESSIONISM

The intent and techniques of expressionism are in direct opposition to Kammerspiel. It is the reverse side of man's psychological nature. Expressionism externalizes Kammerspiel's delicate interior drama, overtly exposes its tortured underpinnings and transforms its calm facade and measured symbolism into grotesque graphics and mythic imagery. Kammerspiel utilizes realism and understatement; expressionism utilizes exaggeration and overstatement; but both are dependent upon psychology, often of a complicated nature.

The ego is the essential part of the expressionist's universe; in fact, the universe is his projected ego. No image, if conjured up by the ego, can be too distorted, no plot too implausible, no gesture exaggerated. The expressionists employed every technique, every trick at their disposal to project their ego onto the universe, and cinema, with its endless possibilities for *trompe-l'oeil*, became a natural expressionist medium.

During the period from 1910 to 1920 expressionism became the dominant art force in Germany and, to a lesser extent, Scandinavia. At the height of expressionism there was almost no remnant of its Kammerspiel beginnings; it had become an art unto itself. Although Dreyer was not an expressionist he could

not help but feel the influence of expressionism. Throughout
Dreyer's career, in opposition to Kammerspiel, runs a thread of
"caligarisme," the expressionist techniques perfected by the early
German stage and cinema. German expressionism featured rich
chiaroscuro, jutting and oblique angles, surreal architectonics,
antirealistic sets, and distorted faces—techniques which are
present to a greater or lesser degree in all of Dreyer's films.

Although it appeared well after the crest of German
expressionism, *Vampyr* is Dreyer's only exclusively
expressionistic film. The expressionism seems to have run away
with the Kammerspiel; there is little tension between the two.
Both the subject matter (vampires, afterlife) and the techniques
(chiaroscuro, exaggerated gesture, nonrealistic sets, rampant
fantasy sequences) of *Vampyr* exhibit a confident appreciation of
the strengths of expressionism and a calculated use of its
methods. David Gray, the "protagonist" of *Vampyr*, is not a
Kammerspiel actor whose interior feelings have to be "pushed
out." His feelings are already externalized: he wears them quite
literally on his sleeve, or his staircase, or his coffin. His style is not
one of nuance, but of exaggeration; he is not an individual
personality, but the fluid, human component of a distorted,
expressionist universe. Gray's vampire world is rife with familiar
expressionist visual fetishes: an obsession with darkened
staircases, arching doorways, and vanishing corridors. *Vampyr*
ranks with the greatest of the German expressionist films
(*Nosferatu*, *Metropolis*), and its apparent singularity among

Expressionism in *Vampyr*: "Gray's vampire-world is rife
with familiar expressionist visual fetishes: an obsession with
darkened staircases, arching doorways and vanishing
corridors."

Dreyer's films demonstrates not only his versatility but also his intuitive cinematic genius for varying types of film style. Compared with a doctrinaire Kammerspielfilm like *Master of the House*, it also serves to sow the seeds of stylistic schizophrenia that one senses in Dreyer's films: the uneasy combination of definitely uncongenial styles.

Like Wilhelm Worringer, the German aesthetician whose theories anticipated German expressionism, Dreyer defines what one calls "expressionism" in his films as "abstraction," the reducing of spatial instability into geometric form. "Abstraction allows the director to get outside the fence with which naturalism has surrounded his medium. It allows his films to be not merely visual, but spiritual. The director must share his own artistic and spiritual experiences with the audience. Abstraction will give him a chance of doing it, of replacing reality with his own subjective interpretations."[11] Dreyer seems to be saying quite forthrightly that he consciously uses expressionistic techniques (abstraction) to break out of the fence of Kammerspiel (naturalism); he also states that he feels (like Perrin) that expressionism gives his films their spiritual weight—an assumption which, of course, is under question in this essay. When combined with Kammerspiel, expressionism perfoms a crucial function: it "abstracts" the individual pschology both thematically and visually, transforming it into a common myth. Despite the expressionist theoreticians, I do not feel that expressionism (at least in film) has been able to raise abstraction to the level of transcendental awareness. It may give the inner psychology a corporate or universal quality, but it is still inner psychology. To locate the source of Dreyer's "spiritual values" one has to look to another style.

TRANSCENDENTAL STYLE

Like expressionism, transcendental style in Dreyer's films stems from the Kammerspiel and opposes it. But it also opposes expressionism and its right to control the Kammerspiel. Expressionism is an anathema to transcendental style: it is one of the "screens" Bresson scorns. It "interprets" reality, assigning to it a comprehensible (though irrational) psychological reality. The expressionist world is distorted, unreal, perhaps unendurable, but it is nonetheless understandable because one sees it through certain human eyes, whether they be the actor's, director's, or cameraman's. Expressionism doesn't eliminate the barriers which stand between the spectator and the Holy, it exaggerates them and makes them a value in themselves.

Transcendental style prefers to undermine the Kammerspiel rather than attack it. It does not transform the external world; in stasis the mountain looks pretty much like it did in the everyday. It transforms the rationale of the world without changing its exterior. It does not rely on objective "proof"—whether that be the slight gesture of an actor (Kammerspiel) or a transfigured universe (expressionism)—but on a carefully constructed phenomenology of faith.

Everyday.

The scrupulous attention to day-to-day reality in Dreyer's films, of course, has its origins in Kammerspiele. Motion pictures allowed film-makers to carry even further the realistic tendencies of the nineteenth century, whether in the chamber play or the naturalist novel. Dreyer's use of everyday is not unique: in his earlier films it was a Kammerspiel concern for minor details and seemingly insignificant movements; in his later films it became more ascetic and Bressonesque, resulting in flat empty sets, inexpressive dialogue, natural soundtrack, and long takes.

In many areas one can detect the conflict between transcendental style and Kammerspiel and expressionism. In the Kammerspiel tradition he relies heavily on his actors ("he has to create. I can only stand by"[12]), but in his later films, like Ozu and Bresson, he instructed his actors to "play nothing."[13] Like Ozu and Bresson, Dreyer has a factual concern for faces, but that concern can very easily turn to empathy by nuance (Kammerspiel) or exaggeration (the painted masks of expressionism). If the everyday is able to successfully stylize the Kammerspiel, it then is mitigated by expressionism: Dreyer creates the surface of reality, then seemingly becomes enamored with the surface itself, mistaking the means for the end.

Disparity.

Dreyer's films often feature a character totally estranged from his environment: Joan of Arc, Marthe, the witch in *Day of Wrath*, John, God's fool in *Ordet*. As in Bresson's films these characters have no human metaphorical contact with reality, and their effect on the audience is similarly schizoid. To a large degree this disparity is caused by the tension between Kammerspiel (naturalistic settings) and expressionism (contrived camera composition and angle). Such a stylistic tension explains the protagonist's psychological dilemma, but it does not explain that other tension of which Dreyer speaks: "It is that latent tension, that smoldering discomfort behind the minister's family's everyday life that I have so urgently been trying to bring forward."[14] This disparity (the Other within the physical) is the disparity of transcendental style. Dreyer not only creates disparity in the conventional psychological sense by contrasting Kammerspiel and expressionism, but he also creates disparity in the manner of transcendental style by designing a character like John in *Ordet* who has no psychological (interior or exterior) cause for his estranging passion, a character who is truly the "fool of God."

In the case of *Ordet* the disparity is confirmed with the definitive decisive action, the raising of the dead. This unexpected miracle within a dour Nordic universe is quite consciously "shocking," and consequently demands some sort of pro or con commitment from the spectator. Within the context of Dreyer's varied styles the resulting effect of this miracle may not be what transcendental style prescribes, but the concept of a miraculous event within a carefully constructed banal reality is much more a part of transcendental style than Kammerspiel or expressionism.

Stasis.

Dreyer's lack of commitment to the transcendental style becomes most apparent in his failure to achieve stasis. Some of Dreyer's statements ("We hope that film will set ajar for us a door into other worlds"[15]) as well as his partial use of everyday and disparity indicate that he genuinely desired to create transcendental art, although the nonstasis endings of his films, as we shall see, suggest other intentions. Whatever Dreyer's true intentions were (and I tend to think they were mixed), he was never able to achieve stasis, the final test of transcendental art, to the extent that Ozu and Bresson did because, it seems to me, he never relied on the transcendental style to the extent that they did. When the final moment of would-be stasis occurred, Dreyer had hedged his bets, leaving elements of Kammerspiel untouched and intertwining expressionism with transcendental style, thereby offering the viewer alternative explanations, spiritual and psychological, for the decisive action.

Like many artists with spiritual intentions Dreyer uses the "frozen image," but it is crucial to ask what he is freezing. Is he freezing the commitment which comes after the decisive action, or is he freezing the disparity itself, creating an endless syndrome of earthly struggle?

Because Dreyer increasingly used elements of transcendental style in his films, one may suggest that he was progressing toward a thesis-antithesis-synthesis/ Kammerspiel-expressionism-transcendental style evolution. Although a late Dreyer Kammerspiel film (*Gertrud*) has more of the ascetic elements of transcendental style than an early one (*Master of the House*), Dreyer, as far as one can ascertain, rejected complete stasis to the very end of his career. Before positing an explanation why Dreyer did not choose to create stasis, it will be helpful to examine how Kammerspiel, expressionism, and transcendental style interrelate in three specific films.

THE PASSION OF JOAN OF ARC

A comparison between Dreyer's and Bresson's Joan of Arc films is not only convenient but also fruitful, explicitly establishing their different attitudes toward hagiography. Dreyer's film is a passion;* Bresson's is a trial. Both depict the historical Joan, but whereas Dreyer emphasizes, in Bazin's terms, the psychology of her existence, Bresson emphasizes the physiology of her existence. Both Joans are alienated, but whereas Dreyer's Joan is reactive to her social surroundings, Bresson's Joan is a solitary soul, responding primarily to her voices. Both films reveal the sainthood of Joan: Dreyer through her humanity, Bresson through her divinity. Both view Joan as a suffering intercessor between God and man: Dreyer as the crucified, sacrificial lamb, Bresson as the resurrected, glorified icon.

* The passion of Dreyer's *The Passion of Joan of Arc* is different from the Passion I have associated with transcendental style, that is, the holy agony. Dreyer's passion is physical, psychological, and spiritual suffering, whereas Bresson's is almost exclusively spiritual.

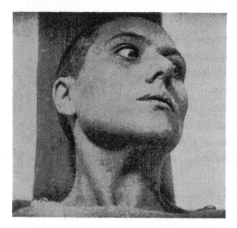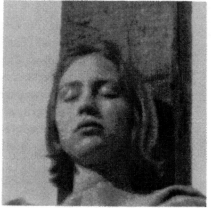

Joan at the moment of death, as visualized by Dreyer, left, and
Bresson, right: "Both view Joan as a suffering intercessor between
God and man: Dreyer as the crucified, sacrificial lamb, Bresson as the
resurrected, glorified icon."

This theological distinction carries over into direction and
camera techniques. Dreyer and Bresson both employ the
transcendental style, but whereas Dreyer weights the style
heavily with Kammerspiel and expressionism, Bresson uses it
exclusively.

In *The Passion of Joan of Arc* expressionist detail is
evident in choice of subject, composition, camera movement, and
staging. Characters in expressionist films often wore masks or
heavy face paint to obscure their individual identities and merge
them with the distorted expressionist decor. The faces in Dreyer's
Passion, although seemingly "documentary" because of their lack
of make-up, become their own "masks." Dreyer's obsession with
"wrinkles" soon surpasses the psychological concerns of the
chamber play and comes to resemble the expressionist mania for
distortion. Each face contains a wealth of detail: craggy ridges,
puffy cheeks, bulbous eyebrows, sclerotic warts, globes of sweat;
Dreyer's close-up camera accentuates every facial aberration,
every "nuance" of expression. The faces of Joan's inquisitors are
genuinely oppressive, and part of Joan's fear and trembling comes
from the Expressionist tradition: an innocent female victim
trapped and terrorized by ghastly demonic distorted faces. The
antagonistic faces of the judges are active; they attack the
defenseless and submissive Joan whose passive face receives and
reflects their emotional aggression.

For Dreyer the function of these distorted faces, as for expressionism, is to create audience empathy—both pity and fear—for Joan: "The result of the close-ups was that the spectator was as shocked as Joan was, receiving the questions, tortured by them. And, in fact, it was my intention to get this result."[16] Dreyer's use of faces is diametrically opposed to Bresson's, which actively spurns audience empathy. In his only recorded comment on Dreyer's *Passion*, Bresson stated, "I understand that at the time this film was a small revolution, but now I only see all the actors' horrible buffooneries, terror-stricken grimaces which make me want to flee."[17]

The composition and sets of *Passion* serve the same purpose as the faces: they offer an expressive environment in which the viewer can emotionally participate. This environment also permits the viewer to read-in character psychology which may not be explicit in the film. The receding arches, each with its separate shadow, give the corridors an emotional weight of their own, and as Joan moves unwillingly through them she acquires that weight. The architecture of Joan's world literally conspires against her; like the faces of her inquisitors, the halls, doorways, furniture are on the offensive, striking, swooping at her with oblique angles, attacking her with hard-edged chunks of black and white. The torture chamber sequence, in particular, is a familiar piece of expressionism; its horror comes not so much from its ability to inflict pain but from its demented chiaroscuro and sinister obliquity.

The expressionistic architecture is implemented by the camerawork. In *Passion* Dreyer's camera is not stationary like Ozu's or Bresson's, but is hyperactive, taking as many as four or five vantage points in a single scene. Dreyer's emotive intentions are often obvious: again and again he dollies down that long ominous line of oppressive faces, and cuts quickly, on motion, to a stationary shot of Joan's upturned, suffering face. Not only is poor Joan being attacked by the judges, the architecture, the lighting, but even the camera movement is conspiring against her. Dreyer's use of camera angle is also unabashed: Joan is usually seen from a high angle as contrasted with the judges who are shot from a long angle. A shot of the reflection pool in which soldiers are seen running is less obvious in its intent, but like the low angle it serves a fundamental purpose: to create a directoral screen

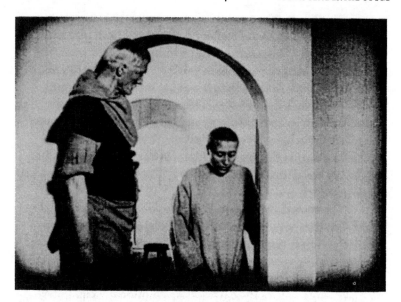

The Passion of Joan of Arc: "The receding arches, each with its separate shadow, give the corridors an emotional weight of their own, and as Joan moves unwillingly through them she acquires that weight."

between the viewer and the event, a screen which will help place the event in time, space, emotion, and effect.

But *The Passion of Joan of Arc* is much more than a chamber play with an overlay of expressionism, like the German expressionist films *Nju* or *The Treasure*, it also has that "other" quality. *Passion* also contains some of the elements of transcendental style. When unhampered by expressionist camerawork, there is a detached examination of detail, such as the shot of the blood spurting from Joan's arm. Like Bresson, Dreyer opens his film with the shot of a ledger which details the factual, recorded evidence of the trial. In a manner very similar to Bresson, Dreyer allows the camera to linger on a scene after the "action" has passed: Joan enters the frame, opens the door, exits, and the camera holds on the closed door. The extensive use of close-up and lack of make-up also establish the everyday. On several occasions viewers have remarked that they thought *Passion*, a silent film, was better without musical accompaniment than with. The reason, I think, is that without music there is more everyday; there is one less screen to interfere with the spiritual progress of Joan's soul. When a viewer sees a close-up of the jailer's key opening Joan's cell, he can hear the rattling in his mind, and the meticulous sense of everyday reality is reinforced.

The causes of Joan's disparity also seem deeper than just a conflict between Kammerspiel and expressionism, between simple life and distorted detail. Joan reacts emotionally to her hostile environment, but she also reacts spiritually to an external dimension. She does not only see her inquisitors as political pawns or demonic gorgons (as the camera sees them), but she also considers them representatives of the other world sent to torture and test her. She accuses them of being emissaries of the devil, and although her reasons seem to stem primarily from the expressionism-induced paranoia, they also stem from a genuine and overwhelming spiritual passion. She professes her faith quite simply and straightforwardly, and although her fear may come from the hostile surroundings, her faith does not. These elements of transcendental style—factual examination, overemphasis on detail in the door opening/closing scenes, an incredible faith— consistently suggest a spiritual weight in *The Passion of Joan of Arc*.

In the final test of transcendental style, stasis, however, Dreyer remains uncommitted to either psychology or spirituality, expressionism or transcendental style, and Dreyer's lack of commitment begets a similar lack of commitment in the spectator—stasis is not achieved. Dreyer uses his codas not for stasis, as Ozu and Bresson do, but to place the action in a social context. After a particularly grueling interrogation, Dreyer cuts away from Joan and focuses either on the reaction of the judges or the mobs gathered outside. The viewer feels pity for Joan, but that pity never leads to anything foolish (like belief) because the viewer continually is also given the perspective of uncommitted spectators. Thus when the supposed decisive action occurs— Joan's martyrdom—the viewer can evaluate it from a detached position, interpreting it either psychologically or sociologically. In his comparison of the two Joan of Arc films Jean Sémolué notes this crucial difference: "In *The Trial of Joan of Arc* each spectator adheres solitarily to the solitary agony of the heroine. In *The Passion of Joan of Arc* the flesh of a martyr interceding for us is beautified . . . we, the spectators, are represented by the crowd, we become, through our intermediary, actors in the drama, like the kneeling donors of a medieval tableau, hands folded and faces bathed with tears."[18] Sémolué intends this to be complimentary toward *Passion* (and, indeed, it is complimentary, although not in the sense of transcendental style), but it also demonstrates that Dreyer by premeditating the Transcendent on emotional empathy deprives himself of the spiritually elevating effect of transcendental style. Dreyer's viewers are perpetually stuck at the foot of the cross, weeping over a corpse soon cold, whereas Bresson's viewers may have transcended the veil of tears, passing on to something more permanent and edifying.

Any attempts Dreyer may have made at stasis collapse in the final moments of *Passion*. Joan's martyrdom is thrown into the simmering social context: the crowd turns to riot, the soldiers forcibly suppress them, killing and injuring many. This sequence is filmed in an empathy evoking manner; the footage is action-cut and the soldiers are seen á la expressionism through grated bars from overhead. If he had any doubts, the last sequence takes the viewer off the transcendental hook. He may interpret Joan's death psychologically, sociologically, or spiritually, and given such a choice the viewer's natural preference is for either of the first two. The closing shots of the Dreyer and Bresson Joan of Arc films are ironically dissimilar. After the riot following Joan's death, Dreyer cuts back to the charred stake and pans upward, attempting artificially to force the viewer's thoughts heavenward while they actually remain on the chaos below. Bresson has no riot; her death is as perfunctory as her life. His also ends with a shot of the charred stake, but does not pan upward. The viewer's attention remains earthbound, but his soul, as dictates the transcendental style, theoretically soars upward.

The sociological ending of *Passion* justifies the interpretations of the film as a study of Joan the woman,[19] and as a film which reveals Dreyer's attitude toward women.[20] Such interpretations are viable because Dreyer does not, like Bresson, eschew arguments based solely on personality. In either case we move further away from transcendental style and toward the familiar, comprehensible terrain of expressionist and psychological cinema.

DAY OF WRATH

Day of Wrath also lends itself to analysis; it seemingly splits right down the middle: one-half predominantly transcendental style, the other half predominantly expressionist/psychological. Robert Warshow was probably the first critic to recognize what is described in this essay as "transcendental style." In a 1948 essay entitled *"Day of Wrath*: The Enclosed Image" Warshow described the dualistic quality of Dreyer's film. Warshow praised the first half (transcendental style), yet felt it was necessarily doomed to failure, as exemplified by the second half (expressionism). Dreyer's failure in *Day of Wrath* became prescriptive for any film attempting to evoke the spiritual dimension: "the camera," Warshow wrote," cannot create a religious system."[21] Dreyer was the first director to seriously raise the possibility of creating a "religious system" on film, and his particular difficulties were naturally attributed to the enormity of his task. But the failings of *Day of Wrath* stem more from Dreyer than from the style which would in other hands come remarkably close to creating a religious system—as close, in fact, as any work of art has come.

The first half of *Day of Wrath* concerns Herlof's Marthe, an old woman who is condemned as a witch, hunted down, tortured, tried and burned at the stake. Marthe is the nether side of Joan of Arc—the Transcendent seen through a demonic mirror. Like Joan, her fate is predetermined (written out by official decree on the outset of the film), her inquisitors are narrow-minded, her confession is extracted through torture, and, most importantly, she responds viscerally to a nonhuman, spiritual force. But unlike Joan, Marthe is old, misshapen, spiteful, conniving, and her "martyrdom" and "purification" are supposedly in service to Satan. (Although, crucially, Dreyer does not make a moral judgment on deviltry; it is not "evil." The characters of *Day of Wrath* assume that witchcraft is evil, but Dreyer treats it in the same affecting manner he treats sainthood in *Passion*. He seems more interested in the Transcendent than with moral judgments.)

Warshow's comments about this section of *Day of Wrath* prefigure many of the comments Sontag was to later make about Bresson. The music ("Dies Irae"), Warshow wrote, "does not aim at the listener's pleasure or require his consent." He points

Decisive action in the first half of *Day of Wrath*: the death of Herlof's Marthe. "Marthe is the nether side of Joan of Arc—the transcendent seen through a demonic mirror."

out that there is no "dramatic conflict" surrounding the witch "yet this formalized and narrow spectacle creates a degree of excitement beyond anything one experiences during the later, more dramatic portions of the film." Warshow continues, "It is as if the director, in his refusal to acknowledge that physical movement implies dramatic movement, were denying the relevance of the spectator's feelings; one is left with no secure means of connecting the witch with reality, and yet she is real in herself and must be responded to; as responses are blocked, the tension increases." And, even more crucially, he states, "The feelings of the spectator really are in a way irrelevant: he is watching what has ceased to exist, and there is no one to care what he feels. He has feelings nevertheless."

The similarity of the comments by Warshow, Sontag, and Ayfre underline the thesis of this essay—that "spiritual" directors like Ozu, Bresson, and Dreyer were not only similar in intent but in means, that there was a common style they drew on to achieve similar effects. Transcendental style in *Day of Wrath* seems a more precise explanation for the film's spiritual depth than Kammerspiel or expressionism, neither of which is normally known for their spiritual qualities.

The Marthe section of *Day of Wrath* is a remarkably straightforward use of the everyday-disparity-statis formula. The everyday and disparity are created in the manner of *The Passion of Joan of Arc* (the spiritual obsession within the cold reality), but the decisive action in *Day of Wrath*, unlike *Passion*, is not mitigated by social events and has a genuine force. As Marthe's screaming body is lifted into the flames one senses that something Other Worldly has been destroyed. This is primarily because the sudden emotional release of her martyrdom functions as the decisive action, forcing the viewer to accept or reject the disparity prior to it. The decisive action breaks the everyday stylization thematically (total emotional release) and technically (the introduction of a vertical line into a previously horizontal composition). This "decisive" effect of Marthe's martyrdom was calculated by Dreyer: "As a principal rule one can say that one shall try to keep a continuous, flowing, horizontally gliding motion in the film. If one then suddenly introduces vertical lines, one can by this reach an instantly dramatic effect—as, for instance, in the pictures of the vertical ladder just before it is thrown into the fire in *Day of Wrath*."[22]

Warshow points out both the everyday ("there is no one to 'care' ") and the disparity ("he has feelings nevertheless"), but he passes over stasis—for the obvious reason that Dreyer himself passes over it. *Day of Wrath* continues and the Marthe episode becomes the stimulus for a new expressionist/psychological drama. Anne (the wife of Absalom, one of Marthe's judges) contracts witchcraft through contact with Marthe. The focus of the film switches from witchcraft itself to the psychology of witchcraft. The central question of the first half of the film is, "Are there such things as witches?" The central question of the second half is, "Why does Anne think she is a witch?" Anne's witchcraft is not caused, like Marthe's, by some transcendent source, but by intense psychological pressure.

Anne married the elderly, dour Absalom out of obligation, but she falls in love with his son Martin, who has returned from the seminary. Anne and Martin attempt to hide their love, romancing only on clandestine field trips. This conflict is reflected in the decor: the parsonage is claustrophobic and chiaroscuric; the fields are bucolic and well-lit. The dilemma of this section is, as Anne says, "Is it a sin to love?" This dilemma is resolved by the

Anne in *Day of Wrath*: "Dreyer makes her look
'witchy' by using chiaroscuro close-ups; her face is
often blocked half in light, half in dark."

introduction of witchcraft into Anne's life. Marthe had told her
that Anne's mother was also a witch, and now Anne begins to
feel this power. She wishes Absalom dead and after a near miss,
she succeeds: Absalom has a heart attack. The central question of
the second half of *Day of Wrath* then shifts from whether or not
love is legitimate (and it obviously is) to whether persons under
intense psychological pressure can have delusions of witchcraft.

Anne's witchcraft, as opposed to Marthe's, seems to be the
result of psychological tensions. Dreyer makes her look "witchy"
by using chiaroscuric close-ups. Her face is often blocked half in
light, half in dark; the candles beside Absalom's coffin flicker in
her eyes. As Anne is being questioned there is a double exposure
on her face of the shifting pattern of leaves which also appeared
on Marthe's face before she was burnt. Dreyer also employs overt

symbolism, associating the powers of witchcraft with thunderstorms and lightning. The expressionistic techniques which are prevalent throughout the film now seem to bear directly on Anne's disintegrating mind. For Anne, witchcraft is a psychological delusion, the direct result of her forbidden love. After Absalom's death she says, "I believe he died for our sake." Martin replies, "Did you wish him dead?" and Anne says, "I love you. That is my only crime."

Absalom's "miraculous" death is not rational, but it is understandable: it is the expression of Anne's psychosis. In the second half of *Day of Wrath* the decisive action (Absalom's death) does not happen to the protagonist, but is used to give the viewer a detached perspective of the protagonist. After Absalom's death the spectator may be convinced of the reality and immediacy of Anne's psychosis, but he is unlikely to believe in a supernatural force.

Although both styles are consistently present in *Day of Wrath*, the first half seems primarily transcendental style, the second half primarily expressionism. Perhaps this is because Dreyer considered the first half exposition and characterized Marthe one-dimensionally to set the stage for Anne's trauma. Marthe is tortured in a "chamber of horrors" sequence and this expressionist environment could be seen as responsible for her witchcraft, although Marthe's steadfast protests of innocence help make the environment reflect more on her tormentors than on herself. In any case, the crucial fact that Marthe's witchcraft and not her personality is "at stake" allows the elements of transcendental style to operate in a less encumbered manner during the first half of the film.

Analyzing both sections of the film Warshow concludes, "The attempt to impose belief by purely aesthetic means is inevitably a failure, both dramatically and visually." Yet Warshow derives his arguments from the second half of the film (the symbolic "evil" storm, the double-exposure on Anne's face) and applies them to the entire film. Warshow opposes transcendental style in principle, as every healthy skeptic should, but he takes his proof texts from the expressionist sections of *Day of Wrath*. Warshow is correct, however, in his implication that stasis is never achieved; the conflict between internal and external rationale is never resolved, or even confronted.

ORDET

Many of the elements of transcendental style are explicit
in *Ordet*. Of all Dreyer's films, *Ordet* comes the closest in
technique and effect to the work of Ozu and Bresson. Dreyer's
Ordet is the second screen version of Kaj Munk's play. The first,
filmed by Swedish director Gustav Molander in 1943, gave
Munk's play a realistic, rational interpretation; the "miracle of
Kaj Munk," Boerge Trolle wrote of the Molander *Ordet*, "was
interpreted as a return to sanity, capable of scientific explanation
but nevertheless appearing miraculous to those directly in contact
with it."[23]

Dreyer's adaptation is obviously antithetical to
Molander's.* In *Ordet*, as in no other Dreyer film, one senses the
self-conscious use of transcendental style. Expressionism
seemingly plays no role in *Ordet*: transcendental style operates
from within the Kammerspiel and is given little "competition"
from expressionism. In many ways *Ordet* is a conventional
Kammerspielfilm: the action takes place primarily indoors, within
a fixed number of rooms and among fixed groups of individuals.
Certain scenes and conversations are repeated, expanded, refined
until certain psychological truths are revealed. The sets are
naturalistic; there is no exaggeration in lighting, camerawork,
or acting.

---

* What seems obvious to the viewer of *Ordet*, however, may not have been
so obvious to Dreyer. Reacting to a statement by Guido Aristarco that he
had "[rejected] science for the miracles of religion," Dreyer stated that
"The new science brings us toward a more intimate understanding of the
divine power and is even beginning to give us a natural explanation to
things of the supernatural. The John figure of Kaj Munk's can now be seen
from another angle . . . I have not rejected modern science for the miracle
of religion. On the contrary, Kaj Munk's play assumed new and added
significance for me, because the paradoxical thoughts and ideas expressed
in the play have been proved by recent psychic research . . . explained the
seemingly inexplicable happenings of the play and established a natural
cohesion behind the supernatural occurrences that are found in the film"
("Letter," *Film Culture*, No. 7 [1956], p. 24). Dreyer's statement does not
alter the fact that his *Ordet* is undeniably more "mysterious" and more
"miraculous" than Molander's; but it does reinforce the contention of this
essay that Dreyer's thinking was intentionally dualistic. He would not
give up the scientific for the miraculous, just as he would not give up the
miraculous for the scientific.

But the techniques of transcendental style go beyond the Kammerspiel, formalizing its naturalistic elements. The sets and lighting in the chamber plays, although not distorted as in the expressionist plays, were very expressive, correlating nuances of emotion with nuances of set design and chiaroscuro. In *Ordet*, however, the sets are often stark and the lighting toneless. In contrast to the previous Dreyer films, many of the scenes are shockingly one-dimensional; the characters recite their lines before a blank backdrop set at a 90° angle to the camera. The composition is generally static, permitting the characters to act out an event within a fixed frame; likewise the takes are long, allowing time for a character to walk the full distance of a room and engage in a conversation without a cut. These are the familiar techniques of everyday: by subrogating the empathetic qualities of natural life and formalizing its factual detail, everyday creates a cold stylization.

The "saint" of *Ordet* is John, a man so totally alienated from his environment that he is considered crazy. He is the "fool of God." He makes no secret of either his true identity or his purpose: "I am Jesus of Nazareth," he states, "People believe in the dead Christ but not the living. I have come back to bear witness in Heaven and perform miracles." John is such an obvious "Christ symbol" that it is a shock when Dreyer, with counter-strategy, subtly makes him something more: an actual reincarnated Christ of a later age. The other characters of *Ordet* realize that John is "closer to God" than they themselves, yet until the decisive action they only treat him as a symbol.

John's madness is disguised divinity. Like Joan and Marthe he reacts primarily to the supernatural, not his surroundings; like Joan and Marthe he is "persecuted" (in this case, mocked) for it. His disparity is the country priest's; he is a victim of the holy agony totally unable to respond to his cold environment. Madness replaces martyrdom, it is the last refuge of the saint who must remain within the prisonhouse of the body.

No other explanation for John's madness is given in the body of the film. John's old father, Marten, gives a possible explanation, "he was driven crazy by the study of Kierkegaard," but this reflects more on the father's dunderheaded attitude toward others than it does on his son. John is not the product

of an oppressive, distorted environment as Joan, Anne, and to
a lesser extent Marthe are. His surroundings seem quite sane
and commonplace, quite everyday; he is the only oddity in it.
John's straightforward pronouncements, his inexpressive face,
his overwhelming religious obsession, his inability to function in
a pragmatic world, all mark him as a product of disparity.

Just as John's madness is disparity par excellence, so his
miracle is a decisive action par excellence. In a "Lazarus" scene
he raises his dead sister-in-law Inger from the dead. There is
no coyness or trickery; John commands her to rise from her
coffin and she does. The miracle is unexpected, implausible,
and demands commitment from the spectator.

It is at the stage of stasis, however, in *Ordet* as in Dreyer's
other films, that transcendental style is clearly shown to be only
a part of Dreyer's film-making. John's decisive action partially
elicits a spiritual commitment from the viewer (more, I think,
than any other Dreyer film), but it does not result in a lasting
stasis. One could fault Dreyer for this failure, saying the decisive

Disparity in *Ordet*: John, the fool of God. "John's straightforward
pronouncements, his inexpressive face, his overwhelming religious
obsession, his inability to function in a pragmatic world, all mark him
as a product of disparity."

action was just too drastic to induce belief, but I think this "failure" was intentional. Like Ozu and Bresson, Dreyer uses elements of everyday and disparity, but he shows no inclination to create stasis as they did.

In a film of transcendental style one would expect that the character who experiences the disparity and makes the decisive action would be the central character; it is his disparity which must result in stasis. But John is not the central character of *Ordet*. He is used as an allegorical figure, representing what the other characters must come to believe. In the opening scene he states: "I am a prophet in God's sight. Woe unto every one who believeth not. I am the light of the World, but the darkness apprehendeth it not. I have come unto my people but they have not received me." "His people," his family, at first reject him. His brother Michael states, "Miracles don't happen these days." John repeatedly predicts death, but he is ignored. As Inger lies ill John again predicts her death and states that he can perform a miracle, but a visiting vicar counters that "Miracles don't happen nowadays." John finally receives the power to perform the miracle when Inger's daughter Anne believes in him. After Inger's resurrection the family seems to come to an acceptance of John and all he represents—the living Christ, miracles, disparity, madness. Talking with John after Inger's death Michael had said, "How can one tell madness from sense." And John replied, "You are coming closer."

At this juncture one might think that *Ordet* was using a roundabout version of transcendental style, that the characters of the film, like the viewers, had to gradually realize that John was the central figure. But after his miracle, John again becomes a minor character. The emphasis shifts from John's divinity back to Inger's corporeality. Before the miracle Michael, in response to the consolation that Inger's soul was in heaven, had stated "but I loved her body too." Immediately after her resurrection, Inger, now sitting up in her coffin, kisses Michael at great length and very sensuously. Then Inger, in the last line of the film, says, "Now we begin to live." There is even a hint at this point that John, now with a contented smile on his face, has become sane again. For a spiritually obsessed character like John this is the opposite of martyrdom and sainthood; like Inger, he has been recycled back into life. Dreyer uses the decisive action to reaffirm humanity; it does not disembody the passion, it reembodies it.

The relative absence of expressionism from *Ordet* allows one to see the interreaction between Kammerspiel and transcendental style. The ending of the film indicates that *Ordet* is probably a psychological drama, a Kammerspielfilm, at heart. The main characters have learned to overcome their intolerance, reconcile their differences, live more joyfully, and humanize their dour faith. The amazing thing about *Ordet* is that it accomplishes this purpose through a partial use of transcendental style. Through the use of everyday and disparity Dreyer gives *Ordet* a spiritual depth it normally would not have, then he turns this depth back to work on the psychological drama. It is as if Dreyer carefully sets the viewer up for the Transcendent, then reveals the immanent.

Like Bresson, Dreyer values asceticism; he has never questioned the need for suffering as a means to revelation. Dreyer also, like Bresson, often structures his asceticism within the prison metaphor. The prison metaphor in Western theology leads to death, the separation of the body and soul, but whereas in Bresson death leads to iconography, the disembodied soul, in Dreyer death becomes reincarnation, the new body—Joan's death creates social upheaval, Marthe's death affects Anne, Inger's death leads to rebirth. Dreyer does not want stasis; he seems to prefer perpetual disparity, the body and soul always alive and in tension.

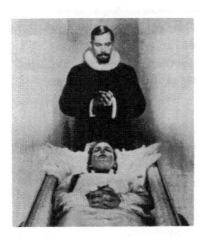

The raising of Inger in *Ordet*: decisive action and retreat from stasis. "It is as if Dreyer carefully sets the viewer up for the Transcendent, then reveals the immanent."

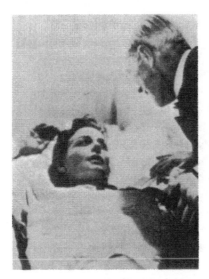

Dreyer's preference for disparity places him in the tradition of Northern European art and theology, just as Bresson's striving for stasis places him in the Southern European Byzantine tradition. A brief glance at an analogous art form, Gothic architecture, as defined by its chief aesthetician, Wilhelm Worringer, will help explain Dreyer's fundamental dualism and its relation to his films.

GOTHIC ARCHITECTURE

Because Dreyer employs, to varying degrees, transcendental style, the prison metaphor, and religious subject matter, there is a natural tendency to equate his films with Bresson's and by association with Byzantine painting, as Perrin does.[24] But the differences between Dreyer and Bresson run as deep as their similarities; they had contrasting conceptions of the Transcendent and how it can be expressed in life and art. Dreyer's films are only similar to Byzantine iconography to the extent that they are similar to Bresson's films. The unique quality of Dreyer's films is close to another form of religious art—Gothic architecture. Dreyer is different from Bresson in many of the same ways the Gothic is different from the Byzantine.

The metaphor of Gothic architecture provides a convenient comparison between Bresson and Dreyer. In principle Gothic architecture is like Bresson's films; in practice it is like Dreyer's. The Scholastic premise of Gothic architecture, as defined by Coomaraswamy, Maritain, and Panofsky, is similar to that of Byzantine art and Bresson's films; the techniques of the actual Gothic cathedrals, particularly the later ones, as defined by Worringer, are similar to those of expressionism and Dreyer's films. Gothic architecture in Dreyer's films, like Zen art in Ozu's or Byzantine portraiture in Bresson's, provides a metaphor which both enlightens without limiting and relates a contemporary artist to an earlier form of religious art. The Gothic cathedral can only be a metaphor; the experience of a cathedral is fundamentally different from the experience of cinema, and what works in one may not work in the other. The Gothic metaphor is a generalization, of course, and for every generalization there is an army of exceptions, but perhaps it will be helpful.

Wilhelm Worringer's early books (*Abstraction and Empathy*, 1907; *Form in Gothic*, 1912) were major works of reevaluative aesthetics; they summarized everything that had been previously thought, criticized it, and posited a new way of thinking. Worringer was one of the first and most important theorists of abstract form in art. In an art world slowly awakening from the spell of realism he championed Oriental, Gothic, and modern art. Although he did not use the term "expressionism," his theories became an integral part of expressionist canon. Quite briefly, Worringer divided art into two categories: "naturalism" and "style." Naturalism was the art of sensuousness; it evoked (in Theodor Lipps' term) "empathy." "Style" was the art of tension; it resulted in "abstraction." Naturalism was the product of a contented, earthbound culture; it was characterized by realistic portraiture and soft lines. The style of abstraction was the result of discontent, the striving for the spiritual; it was characterized by ideal portraiture and harsh angular or perpendicular lines. Only abstraction was a "style," Worringer felt, naturalism was "organic and true to life." Only through abstract style could man express the Transcendent: "For these abstract forms, liberated from all finiteness, are the only ones, and the highest, in which man can find rest from the confusion of the world picture."[25]

For Worringer, both Byzantine and Gothic art were "styles." Both desired to escape the temporal world through abstraction; both rejected empathy as the basis for art. Worringer realized that Southern European art (represented by Byzantine art and, before it, Oriental art) was more "sublime" than Northern European art (late Gothic) although his personal preference tended toward the Nordic:

> The difference between the expressionless, abstract line of Oriental man and the intensified expression of the abstract line of Gothic man is just the difference between a final definitive dualism, born of a most profound insight into the world, and a provisional dualism of a still undeveloped stage of knowledge; that is to say, the difference between the sublime quietism of old age and the exalted pathos of youth.[26]

It is easy to see how Worringer's theory of tension of abstraction
was extended to the German expressionist cinema, even
though he probably would have disapproved of the blatant
empathy-inducing devices of many of the expressionist films.

Northern Gothic architecture resulted from theological
as well as artistic tensions. Although rooted in the conventions
of medieval art, it anticipated the impending Renaissance. The
Gothic tension is the tension between Florence and Byzantium;
it results when man is placed at the center of God's unchanging
universe. Gothic art had two poles: the ideal order of God's
universe, and the changing existence of each person who feels
the pain of past and present.

During the Gothic period, the concept of transcendence
came to incorporate both humanism and pantheism. "Belief in
the absolute transcendence of God then [early Middle Ages],"
art historian Arnold Hauser writes, "involved a depreciation of
nature, just as now [Gothic art] the prevalent pantheism
brought about its rehabilitation. . . . The essential change is
that the one-sidedly spiritual art of the early Middle Ages, which
rejected all imitation of directly experienced reality and all
confirmation by sense, has given way to an art that makes all
validity of statement, even about the most supernatural, ideal
and divine matters, depend upon achieving a far-going
correspondence with the natural sensible reality."[27] In sum,
Gothic art was, Wylie Sypher writes, "the revenge of the person
upon the inhumanity of the Romanesque ikon."[28]

This fundamental dualism of Gothic, Worringer
contended, was neither resolved nor transcended (as in Oriental
art); it remained perpetually in conflict. "Its essential nature,"
he wrote, "seems to be far more that of a restless urge which in
its quest for rest, its seeking for deliverance, can find no
satisfaction but that of stupefaction, of intoxication. And thus the
dualism . . . resolves itself into a confused mania of ecstasy."[29]
And "to express ecstasy," Emile Malle concluded in his study of
medieval art, "Gothic art made use of all its incantations, all its
magic of light and shadow. Religious art had never attempted
anything of the kind before; it reached the extreme limit of the
possible."[30]

The late Gothic cathedral is the *reductio ad absurdum*
of the Scholastic method with its *sic* and *non*, its internal

contradictions eternally interlocked: saints and gargoyles, Pantokrators and crucified Christs, oblique lines of force and verticals and horizontals. The lines of tension often clash randomly, lacking focus or climax; Gothic art furnished a dramatic space but not a dramatic focus to which all characters and lines were inevitably drawn. Worringer found in Gothic statuary a microcosm of the Gothic style: the face was often naturalistic, the robe abstract. The body, wrapped in stiff robes, represented the order of Byzantium; the face, often empathic, cried out the humanism of Florence. The inherent contradiction of Gothic life drove the abstract line into near chaos. The impulse of the Gothic man toward true knowledge, Worringer wrote, "being denied its natural satisfaction, thus exhausts itself in wild fantasies . . . everything becomes weird and fantastic."[31] The final solution of Gothic architecture was one of self-negation: instead of defining space, it attacked it; instead of creating order on earth, it thrust instability into the heavens.

Dreyer's films contain the same tensions and contradictions which plagued Gothic architecture. Like the Gothic artist, Dreyer sought a place for spiritual values within corporeality, and like the Gothic artist his search ended in frustration, abstraction, and in some cases, distortion. His films, like the Gothic cathedral, are an unstable equilibrium of world-affirming and world-denying impulses. His films are rife with contradictions: in *Day of Wrath* a stylized martyrdom is followed by pastoral scenes of summer romance; in *Ordet* the ultimate invocation of the Holy is followed by a sensuous kiss. Joan of Arc's struggle to both stay alive and "be with God" is a typically Gothic struggle. Confronted with some of the same problems as the Gothic artist, Dreyer evolved some of the same solutions: obliquity, multiplicity of focal points, contradictory themes.

In his excellent study of structure and composition in Dreyer's films, Philippe Parrain has demonstrated that Dreyer's films are composed on primarily oblique vertical lines which intersect at as many as four points in a single composition. Like the rocketing, crashing lines of a vaulted Gothic cathedral, these oblique verticals keep the eye continually in motion. With certain notable exceptions (such as the everyday scenes in *Ordet*), a solid horizontal line seldom intersects a dominant vertical line in Dreyer's films. Even in a seemingly placid scene the eye cannot rest—there are always tensions between foreground and background, between left-to-right and right-to-left lines of force which compete for attention. This tension can be created by costume design as well as set design and frame composition. In *Day of Wrath*, for example, Merete, Absalom's dour housekeeper, usually wears an enormous seventeenth-century white wing collar. In the dimly-lit indoor scenes (the only ones in which she appears), Merete's collar picks up more light than her face or her surroundings. Her bright V-shaped collar, when extended, forms diagonal, intersecting lines of force in the shape of an X. When further extended, these lines of force go beyond Merete's heavyset, black-robed body and intersecting with the vertical pillars or doorways in the background. Merete may speak commandingly, her tone of voice may demand attention, but the crucial lines of force are leading away from her and do not even intersect on her face. The strident, straightforward nature of Merete's speech conflicts with the attention-draining lines of force and the multiplicity of focal points. This is not the sort of visual tension which contradicts the dialogue or action (as when something is happening in the background antithetical to the foreground), but it undermines it, breaking up its apparent unity.

Oblique orientation, whether in a cathedral or a film, pits large chunks of space against each other. It does not unify or pacify space, it antagonizes it. Oblique orientation presupposes that the artist does not conceive of space as a unity, but rather views every object or part of an object as an independent action within space. Therefore, no character in a frame which is splintered obliquely can speak authoritatively from that space, but must be considered as one of a number of interacting forces.

At times Dreyer's tension even bursts out of the frame. In a well-known composition from *The Passion of Joan of Arc*, a guard, partially hidden by the left vertical frame line, is tugging at Joan's arm while Joan herself is struggling to pull herself outside of the right vertical frame line. The frame line seems an arbitrary restriction on a tension which is on the verge of flying apart. The effect is similar to that which one experiences standing in the nave of a Gothic cathedral as the lines of force explode from the ceiling driving straight through the aisles, through the walls, and out into the flying buttresses. The frame or the nave, the movie or the cathedral themselves, are artistic restrictions upon a reality which by itself would disintegrate.

Dreyer's films and Gothic architecture are both forms of unresolved disparity. Disparity was the definitive quality of Worringer's statues, part stylistic abstraction, part naturalistic empathy. The Gothic counterpart to what this essay has called disparity is exemplified by what Wylie Sypher called the "final achievement of Medieval painting," the Villeneuve-Avignon *Pieta*:

> the anguished stiff body of Christ is bent at an angle full of pathos over the lap of a weeping and mannered Mary . . . in the background, at the left, very small, are the walls and towers of Jerusalem. The sky is vacant bronze. The humanity of these figures is as authentic as anything in Renaissance painting; here are the Gothic *dramatis personae* . . . the Gothic figures are secular, but their world is not. They do not *fit into* a humanized perspective . . . the focus is double, suiting the double Gothic experience of reality—worldly and other-worldly; and the proportions of the scene are alien to the men who inhabit it.[32]

> The guard struggles with Joan in *The Passion of Joan of Arc*: "The frame line seems an arbitrary restriction on a tension which is on the verge of flying apart. The effect is similar to standing in the nave of a Gothic cathedral as the lines of force explode from the ceiling driving through the aisles, through the walls and into the flying buttresses."

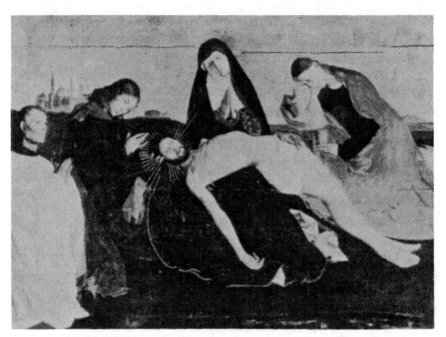

Gothic disparity in the Villeneuve-Avignon Pieta: "The Gothic figures are secular, but their world is not. They do not *fit into* a humanized perspective."

Like the disparity of transcendental style, whether in the films of Ozu, Bresson, or Dreyer, the characters do not *fit into* their environment. But whereas many art styles—Zen, Byzantine, transcendental—have used disparity as a means, Dreyer, like Gothic art, uses it as an end. Dreyer's films and Gothic architecture present man's existential disparity in an agonized, unflinching manner, but stasis seems beyond both their intentions and capabilities. The incomplete and inadequate knowledge disparity provides becomes a virtue in itself, the best a man can hope for.

In Worringer's schema one can find certain similarities between Bresson and Dreyer. Bresson and Dreyer both experience a tension between this world and the next and express this tension through abstraction. Both prefer style to naturalism, abstraction to empathy. But one can find even more crucial differences:

Bresson, like the Byzantine artist, unifies space. He uses Worringer's "inexpressive abstract line" to formalize and pacify the background. Like the Byzantine icon, his frame composition has "a stability which cancels out contradictory movements."[33] In

any given frame from Bresson's films there is most likely to be
only one focal point, and that is the point which best expresses
the tension between the protagonist and his surroundings. Again
and again in Bresson's films the dominant horizontal line meets
the dominant vertical line at a right angle at the protagonist's eyes
or mouth. The viewer's attention is concentrated on the face; it is
there he must read in the tension between the unfeeling
background and the spiritual passion being expressed in the
narration. Bresson unifies space in order to present only one focal
point, one tension, and one confrontation—the confrontation
between the spectator and the Holy. If a viewer responds to
Bresson's films, he must respond at the points Bresson has
predetermined for him. And Bresson's regular, unobtrusive
editing is designed to build up this single confrontation through a
series of frames and scenes.

Compositions by Bresson and Dreyer, Byzantine and Gothic. Below,
Pickpocket; overleaf, *Day of Wrath*. "Bresson unifies space; in any
given frame there is likely to be only one focal point. Dreyer divides
space; the frame often has several focal points and seems restless,
at odds with itself."

Dreyer, like the Gothic artist, divides space. He uses
Worringer's "intensified expression of the abstract line" to
antagonize and sector the elements within the frame. Dreyer's
frame often has several focal points, seems restless, discontented,
and at odds with itself. Dreyer's editing, particularly in *Joan of
Arc*, intensifies this break-up of space; the right-to-left oblique
orientation of one shot may be directly opposed by the
left-to-right orientation of the next shot, and so on in rapid
succession. His films contain both "naturalism" (pastoral scenes,
Day of Wrath) and "style" (chiaroscuric interiors, *Day of
Wrath*), both the inexpressive abstract line (white walls, *Ordet*)
and the expressive abstract line (night interior scenes, *Ordet*),
both humanity in conflict with distorted surroundings (Anne,
Day of Wrath) and spirituality in conflict with factual
surroundings (martyrdom of Marthe, *Day of Wrath*), both
frontality (John, *Ordet*) and agonized visage (Joan, *Passion*), both
the Holy and holy feelings. Each of these tensions can be seen to
have its focal point within any given frame, or between two
frames as they are edited together. Consequently, the viewer is
usually not forced into a single confrontation but given a

multiplicity of responses. The divided space sets no priorities; the viewer is able to respond to any one of equally valid tensions he experiences in the film.

This contrast between Bresson and Dreyer—Byzantine and Gothic—is given a theological depth by Paul Tillich's essay on "Protestant art." Tillich defines the Protestant artist as one who is fixated on the "symbol of the Cross" and cannot find adequate symbols to represent the Resurrection.[34] His art is all tension, conflict and suffering—the continual struggle between world-affirmation and world-denial. The suffering itself becomes an end and the cross is its ultimate symbol. Tillich's "Protestant art" is the art of disparity; it is by extension the art of the Gothic cathedral and the art of Carl Dreyer.

Bresson, on the other hand, is the artist of the resurrection, the artist of stasis. The cross for Bresson is a means to a resurrected end, and he is careful not to confuse the cross and the resurrection. Like Dreyer, Bresson uses suffering through the prison metaphor (the "symbol of the Cross"), but unlike Dreyer, Bresson transforms the prison into a symbol of resurrection. In this manner Bresson is like the Byzantine Christian who, as theologian Henri Daniel-Rops writes, "preferred the theology of Glory to the theology of the Cross."[35] Suffering for Bresson is never more than a stepping-stone to stasis.

Dreyer and Bresson are both great artists, and my intention has not been to place them in the same category, ranking one above the other. If Dreyer had attempted to achieve stasis and failed, then he might be placed a little lower on Bresson's ladder. But his art of disparity is distinct and can stand alone. No art historian would fault Gothic architecture at the expense of Byzantine iconography; each art is great in its own terms. Similarly, the disparity of Dreyer's films is just as immediate and fully realized as the stasis of Bresson's films. As artists, both Bresson and Dreyer are equally accomplished, equally "great."

As transcendental artists, however, they are not equally great. Bresson created an art "more edifying, more permanent," and one can make that difficult distinction through the criterion of transcendental style. Both Bresson and Dreyer had great styles, but only Bresson's was the transcendental style. Bresson's films exemplify transcendental style whereas Dreyer's films use only parts of transcendental style and use them well.

Conclusion

Rocks and Bamboo, Wu Chën, Yüan dynasty.

Throughout

this essay there has been one persistent, overriding assumption: that the transcendental style is the proper method for conveying the Holy on film. This has been assumed, but is it necessarily so? Why do austerity and asceticism stand at the gates of the Transcendent; cannot the Transcendent also be expressed through exuberance and expressionism? Why is Ozu preferred to Mizoguchi, Bresson to Resnais, Dreyer to Bergman?

Jacques Maritain writes, "There is no style *reserved* to religious art, there is no *religious technique*. Anyone who believes in the existence of a religious technique is on the high road to Beuron."* Is not this essay, with its insistence on "transcendental style," on that high road?

This alleged "unique" quality of the transcendental style I have defined should be examined in the light of two pertinent considerations: one, what forms have spiritual expression taken in the past? and two, how do these forms relate to the "new" art of motion pictures? This central question (and its incumbent considerations) inevitably raises theological and aesthetic problems beyond the scope of this essay, and my intention here, as throughout, is not to pretend any "new" aesthetics, but rather to situate my concept of filmic "transcendental style" within some previous theories.

---

* Jacques Maritain, *Art and Scholasticism and the Frontiers of Poetry* (New York: Charles Scribner's Sons, 1962), p. 103. Beuronese art, developed in the monastery at Beuron in the 1860s, was one of the earliest "modern arts, and with its primitive qualities anticipated the paintings of Gauguin, Cezanne, and Kandinsky. Beuronese art, however, locked the expression of spirituality into a single form, allowing no room for change and experimentation. Considering its initially innovative style, it had remarkably little impact on succeeding art forms.

The Spiritual in Art

There are many ways to present the Holy in art; no artist or style has cornered the transcendental market. Although, as Maritain states, there is no specific "religious technique," he also goes on to say that "It is true that not every style is equally suited to sacred art."[1] In any given art some styles are best suited to express the sacred, others the profane; and in film no style is better suited to express the Holy than transcendental style.

What sort of general conclusions can be drawn from the checkered history of sacred art? What do the various expressions of the Transcendent have in common: West African sculpture, Zuni masks, Byzantine ikons, Zen gardens, illustrated medieval manuscripts, Gothic architecture, seventeenth-century meditative verse, morality plays, Rembrandt's paintings, Henry Moore's sculptures? Is there anything in the history of transcendental art which can be extracted, abstracted, defined, and then set against the relatively new medium, motion pictures? What distinctions between the Holy and holy feelings have been made in other art forms and do they apply to cinema?

The primal, most irreducible metaphor for the sacred in art, as I said in the Introduction, is the expression of primitive religion through primitive art. Many of the techniques which have been used throughout history to express the Holy in art originated in primitive art. Sacred art has often seemed to favor primitive techniques: two-dimensionality, frontality, the abstract line, the archetypal character.

As a distinction between the Holy and holy feelings, however, the primitive-classical dichotomy is, at best, only valid in principle; it cannot be applied to either a specific historical period or specific techniques. Recent anthropological studies have revealed that there was a good deal more social convention and intrapersonal intention in primitive art than its first exponents imagined, and that classical art, for all its naturalism, could also be intensely religious. The primitive-classical dichotomy has great importance as a generalization, and one must be careful not to use it as anything more than that.

Neither can the primitive-classical dichotomy be directly applied to artistic techniques. Techniques normally ascribed to primitive (sacred) art have been successfully used for classical (secular) purposes. In the long run of history no individual technique can be ascribed to either the sacred or the profane. *There are no religious techniques.* Byzantine art, for example, maintained that the Holy was revealed through artistic compositions with one focal point, so that the viewer's attention is fixed on the face of the saint; Wassily Kandinsky in his apologia for a "new" primitive art 900 years later wrote that the spiritual could be revealed through a composition with many focus points, so that the viewer could appreciate the "inner relationship" of separate, individual shapes and colors.[2] In another example, seventeenth-century meditative poetry maintained that verse could express the sacred through a didactic proposal, rich description and elaborate metaphor; contemporary poets, on the other hand, who desire to reveal the Transcendent prefer the "split line" and the disjointed metaphor. When applied to film, the question of "religious technique" becomes even more thorny. The abstract, expressionistic line which works so well in Gruenwald's Isenheim Altarpiece may have a completely different effect in a feature-length film; an architectural structure which is effective in three dimensions may fail completely when used on a two-dimensional movie screen. When compared to cinema, these earlier forms of transcendental art, as I stated previously, can only function as metaphors.

Because there are no religious techniques, aesthetic generalizations become important and necessary. A technique or form can only be described as "religious" (or transcendental) when defined in a highly restricted context (Byzantine iconography, *sumi-e* painting); in order to apply the lessons of these individual works to another medium one must rely on generalization. Consequently aestheticians and theologians have continually revised the original primitive-classical dichotomy, each adapting it to his own circumstances, each attempting to keep that important distinction alive and meaningful. Worringer described it as the distinction between "naturalism" and "style"; van der Leeuw as the distinction between "naturalism" and "asceticism." To Aldous Huxley it was the difference between "tradition" and "individual style"; to Benjamin Rowland, Jr., it was the difference between "traditional art" and "nontraditional art." And on and on. Each of these distinctions is to some degree limited because they use artistic techniques to comment on universal principles; the aesthetician must be continually on guard: the techniques change, the principles do not. In attempting to correlate the forms of the spiritual in art I prefer a totally nonartistic metaphor, one which does not rely on artistic techniques, but instead refers to types of "good works."

In *Religion and Culture* (1930) Jacques Maritain described two types of "temporal means," and although they apply primarily to good works, he also uses them in referring to artists and theologians. By extension they can also refer to two general artistic forms, sacred and profane. The first of these temporal means, the abundant means (*moyens temporels riches*), are those which "of their nature demand a certain measure of tangible success."[3] This type of good work sustains life in a depraved world: "It would be absurd to despise or reject them, they are necessary, they are part of the natural stuff of human life." The abundant means are the means of the soldier, laborer, and business man; they are the means concerned with praticality, physical goods, and sensual feelings.

The second means, the sparse means (*moyens temprels pauvres*), are "the proper means of the spirit." "The less burdened they are by matter, the more destitute, the less visible—the more efficacious they are. This is because they are pure means for the virtue of the spirit." The sparse means are not ordered toward tangible success but toward the elevation of the spirit. Being the "proper means of wisdom," they are the means of the poet and philosopher: Mozart, Satie, Rembrandt, Dante, Homer, St. Thomas.

"It must be understood," Maritain writes, "that there is an order and hierarchy of these temporal means." And the sparse means are higher than the abundant means: "the world is perishing of dead weight. It will recover its youth only through poverty of the spirit." Although both means are temporal, the sparse means, forsaking tangible success, are necessarily closer to the Holy. Like transcendental art, the sparse means are means approaching an end: "the closer one gets to the essence of the spiritual, the more do temporal means employed in its service diminish." Both means are necessary but not equal: the abundant means keep the body alive so that the sparse means can elevate the soul. Maritain might describe Bresson's country priest as a man who used abundant means only to sustain his sparse means, and who, when his sparse means approached their end, gave up both temporal means.

Similarly, it is possible to say that sacred art uses both abundant and sparse means. The abundant means sustain the viewer's (or reader's or listener's) physical existence, that is, they maintain his interest; the sparse means, meanwhile, elevate his soul. The abundant means in art correspond to Worringer's "naturalism." These means are sensual, emotional, humanistic, individualistic. They are characterized by soft lines, realistic portraiture, three-dimensionality, experimentation; they encourage empathy. The sparse means in art correspond to Worringer's "style." The sparse means are cold, formalistic, hieratic. They are characterized by abstraction, stylized portraiture, two-dimensionality, rigidity; they encourage respect and appreciation. These opposing means are not segregated categories; they are both present and interwork in any piece of art, particularly sacred works of art.

The artist who wishes to express the Transcendent cannot neglect either the abundant or the sparse means, but he must know their priority. The abundant means must serve to sustain the sparse means, the sparse means must yield to a spiritual awareness. In a Byzantine church the abundant means are those which enclose space and facilitate the liturgy; the sparse means are those which, like the vertical line and iconography, demand veneration. Within the Byzantine ikon itself, the abundant means are the variation of color and realistic gesture of the subsidiary characters; the sparse means are the gold background and frontality of the central character. The ratio of abundant to sparse means, of course, varies greatly from one art form to another.

The ratio of abundant and sparse means can be a measure of the "spirituality" of a work of art. The more a work of art can successfully incorporate sparse means within an abundant society, the nearer it approaches its transcendental "end." It is not a very precise measure, of course, but at least it is universally applicable. It can relate to any human activity, artistic, social, or philosophical. Before applying this clumsy measure to film, however, it will be helpful to make some general statements about the comparative nature of motion pictures.

CINEMA AND THE ARTS: TWO OVERVIEWS

In his study of the Holy in art, Gerardus van der Leeuw traces the history of the major arts from their origins in religious practice to the present secularized state. At its beginnings each art form was one with religion but throughout the centuries progressively suffered a "breakup of unity." The ceremonial religious dance evolved into the *sacer ludus*, the *sacer ludus* subsequently subdivided into bourgeois drama and liturgy, the liturgy in its progressional turn became popularized; throughout history the constant trend of art is from the sacred to the profane. The Renaissance, with its emphasis on naturalness and individual effort, usually takes the rap for the "breakup of unity," but van der Leeuw points out that this trend goes as far back as "the great heretic Akhenaten" who gave Egypt's gods the sculptural faces of his family.[4] Only rarely in the history of art, van der Leeuw contends, have talented artists been able to resist the trend toward secularization and return to the religious origins of art.

Van der Leeuw does not discuss cinema in his study. It is quite crucially the only major art form which does not fit into his schema. Motion pictures were not born in religious practice, but instead are the totally profane offspring of capitalism and technology. If a religious artist in cinema attempts to go back to his origins, he will find only entrepreneurs and technocrats.* When the Holy tries to enter into the cinema, the intrinsically profane art, there are bound to be some unusual consequences— consequences which van der Leeuw did not anticipate.

In his essay "The Ontology of the Photographic Image," André Bazin, unlike van der Leeuw, contends that there never was an original unity between religion and art, and that art (in this case, painting) has always been torn between two ambitions: "one, the primarily aesthetic, namely the expression of spiritual reality wherein the symbol transcended the model; the other,

---

* The premise of the original unity of art and religion has been so strong in art criticism that some writers categorically refused to admit the possibility of a profane art. Twenty years after the invention of motion pictures, Alessandro Della Seta wrote: "Art will then never arise and develop among men unless it has a foundation in religion. Art absolutely profane in origin, art born to satisfy the aesthetic taste of the spectator . . . is unconceivable in human history and has absolutely never existed" (*Religion and Art* [London: T. F. Unwin, 1914], p. 35).

purely psychological, namely the duplication of the world outside."[5] From their beginnings the graphic arts demonstrated both these ambitions: one, the primarily aesthetic, in the Byzantine ikons, the other, purely psychological, in the Egyptian death-masks. "Great artists, of course," Bazin adds, "have always been able to combine the two tendencies."

Like van der Leeuw, Bazin felt that the spiritual in art gradually succumbed to the "duplication of the world outside." Although the "purely psychological" had always existed it did not come into dominance until the Renaissance. "Perspective," he writes, "was the original sin of Western painting," and from that time on the spiritual quality of art steadily diminished.

Each overview, whether monistic like van der Leeuw's or dualistic like Bazin's, holds that the spiritual quality in art suffered its decline at the expense of "realism," the duplication of either external or internal reality. Art has always been excited by the challenge of realism: the bison came off the walls and became sculptures, the sculptures became photographs, the photographs moved. Eventually the artist, in his desire to imitate life, attempted to reproduce physical existence itself, not like the Greeks just to portray the highest sensual form. Victor Frankenstein's mad dream was a Gothic extension of a dream shared by many artists of his age: to *artificially* recreate human life and its external surroundings. The urge to duplicate the external world was accompanied by an urge to duplicate the internal world. The romantic artist scrutinized and dutifully recorded his own feelings; he was accountable to no other reality than his own. The myth of the "artist personality" came into full bloom, resulting in both the psychological picturesque and impression, romantic verse and the psychological novel. Sypher has noted the similarities in nineteenth-century realism and romanticism; the romantic work of art, though verging on total fantasy, was only realism turned outside in.[6]

In their pursuit of reality the arts openly coveted each other. The arts of space envied the arts of time and vice versa. Hogarth created sequential paintings to simulate time; Balzac used meticulous painterly descriptions to evoke space. Each art desired the "realism" another dimension could offer, and the continuing search for an art which could be realistic in both space and time certainly engendered the arts' progressive plunge into reality.

Cinema, the duplicatory art in space and time, changed all this. Sypher's cursory contention that cinema threw every other art into the twentieth century and remained woefully in the nineteenth itself[7] is a crucial idea in the history of film and contemporary art, and one which has yet to be fully explicated. Motion pictures have the immediate sense of reality that the arts had so often prostituted themselves to obtain; their axioms were the unattainable goals of realism. Although there still are realistic heights to attain (holographic cinema, for example), cinema has at least temporarily halted the artistic lust for likeness. If the original sin of painting was perspective, Bazin writes, then "it was redeemed from sin by Niepce and Lumière. In achieving the aims of baroque art, photography freed the plastic arts from their obsession with likeness. Painting was forced, as it turned out, to offer us illusion and this illusion was reckoned sufficient unto art. Photography and the cinema on the other hand are discoveries that satisfy, once and for all and in its very essence, our obsession with realism."[8]

Cinema short-circuited the desire to duplicate external reality—no longer would a painter or novelist strive for the realism cinema inherently offered—and plunged the desire to duplicate internal reality into a deeper, more complex level. Cinema was also, as Hauser wrote, "the final step on the road to profanation."[9] It canonized the human, sensual and profane: it celebrated the realistic properties of the nineteenth century while the other arts went on to explore the twentieth. From its outset cinema exemplified the abundant means. Imitative, representational, experiential, it could produce instant empathy.

This peculiar historical perspective of cinema—its profane origins—can produce a sense of "chronological reverse." In the case of film-makers like Ozu and Bresson, cinema did not become progressively profane, it became progressively sacred. In the history of film Bresson came after Dreyer who came after Lumière; it is as if in the history of painting the Byzantine iconographer came after the Gothic architect who came after Hogarth. In cinema it is possible to say that Bresson, whose films have been compared to ikons, purified and rarefied the work of Dreyer, whose films have been compared to a Gothic cathedral.

Spiritual cinema has had to continually draw away from its potentials; being "abundant" at birth, it had to discover the "sparse."

TRANSCENDENTAL STYLE: ABUNDANT AND SPARSE

Seen in this historical perspective, the techniques of transcendental style come into clearer focus. Transcendental style differs from the previous forms of transcendental art in the same way cinema differs from the previous artistic media. Transcendental style adapts the theory of abundant and sparse means to cinema.

Transcendental style, quite obviously, operates in time; it must sustain the viewers's interest from one to three hours. Consequently transcendental style is not a fixed relationship between abundant and sparse means like sculpture, but a fluid interaction creating a temporal as well as spatial rhythm. It gradually can use less abundant and more sparse means, drawing the viewer from the familiar world to the other world. Transcendental style, therefore, has three steps; it is a progressional relationship. It can have the same effect as that upon a viewer who walks through a Byzantine church, moving from the abundant to the sparse artistic means. In cinema, however, it is the art which moves past the passive viewer; it can take him from abundant to sparse means. One way to determine the "spiritual quality" of a cinematic style, therefore, is to examine the manner in which it disposes of its inherent abundant means and substitutes sparse means.

The transcendentally-minded film-maker finds himself in a unique position: he must properly dispose of a surfeit of abundant means (cinema's inherent "realism"). He cannot ignore or neglect these means, but must turn them to his advantage. Cinema may have freed the other arts from their desire to imitate life, as Bazin and Sypher contend, but it did not free itself. In fact, Bazin writes, cinema thereby acquired new chains to the "obsession with reality." This unique alliance of media and abundant means has its advantages as well as its drawbacks. On one hand spiritual cinema was freed from the need to prostitute itself in order to achieve a sense of "realism." Before the advent of cinema, certain religious artists attempted to first create the illusion of the immanent, then break that illusion, thereby revealing the Transcendent. But, for the most part, these artists spent most of their energy unsuccessfully creating the illusion which they never could successfully "break." Because the transcendentally-minded film-maker already has the illusion at his disposal, he can go immediately to the next stage, attempting to break the illusion. However, the religious film-maker cannot ignore the abundant in the way other artists can. A transcendentally-minded painter like Kandinsky, for example, could functionally ignore the abundant means. For him, the abundant means were given; they were the physical gallery where the spectator stood. The canvas itself could be totally sparse, the interplay of abstract forces. Because the cinema is an imitative art in time it not only creates the abstract painting but the gallery as well; a transcendentally-minded film-maker simply cannot dismiss the abundant means out of hand.

A motion picture, from its first frame, has great potential empathy; one of the functions of transcendental style is to use that empathy as *potential* and keep it at that level. The audience has a natural impulse to participate in actions and settings on screen; a film-maker employing transcendental style can use these given abundant means, this natural empathy, to hold the audience in the theater as he gradually substitutes sparse means for abundant. In transcendental style sparse means are, to a large degree, simply a refusal to use the available abundant means. There is no great need to invent new abstract forms; sparseness can be achieved by gradually robbing the abundant means of their potential. Transcendental style must always ride this thin line: it must use the given abundant means to sustain audience interest, and it must simultaneously reject the empathetic rationale for that interest in order to set up a new priority. And because the abundant potential of films is so great, its rejection can be even greater.

In a film of spiritual intent it is necessary, therefore, to have an everyday and a disparity; there can be no instant stasis. The everyday both adheres to the superficial, "realistic" properties of cinema and simultaneously undermines them. A viewer expects certain immediate gratifications from a film: a sense of verifiable reality, factual surety, comprehensible environment. Everyday provides these minor compensations, but it prevents the empathy which would normally ensue. The "reality" of everyday is so thoroughly stylized that it is unreceptive to the sort of empathy which naturally follows a sense of comprehensible environment. It is a textbook example of the proper use of abundant means in sacred art: the abundant means create an environment (on screen) and an audience (in the theater) in which sparse means can operate.

At the stage of disparity the conflict between abundant and sparse artistic means becomes apparent—and disturbing—to the spectator. This conflict is personified by the protagonist; here is a product of abundant means, a man in realistic human form whose physical needs are like our own, yet whose conduct is a model of sparseness. There is a disparity of artistic means: there are abundant imitative techniques—the protagonist and his surroundings; and there is the cold, sparse stylization which supersedes these techniques. Again, transcendental style uses a minimum of abundant means to sustain a film in which the means are becoming increasingly sparse.

Transcendental style theoretically substitutes sparse means for abundant; just how successful it is in this effort can be determined by the decisive action. It is clearly an abundant means, a dramatic or emotional action which cries out for audience empathy. Yet, if transcendental style is successful, the film will at this late point be so bare, so sparse that an abundant technique will have no context to relate to. In the transformed order of artistic means the empathetic, dramatic device now seems out of place.

Stasis, of course, is the final example of sparse means. The image simply stops. The abundant means have been shown to have little purpose; the sparse means, now dominant, will soon give way to the end of the film. The transcendental style will have, it is hoped, set the viewer in motion, moving from abundant to sparse means, as if proceeding down the aisle of a Byzantine church. When the image stops, the viewer keeps going, moving deeper and deeper, one might say, *into* the image. This is the "miracle" of sacred art. If it occurs, the viewer has moved past the point where any "temporal means" (abundant or sparse) are of any avail. He has moved beyond the province of art.

The above schema, of course, is very rough; it does not allow for the subtle interplay of abundant and sparse means which enables the transcendental style to sustain a level of interest over a period of several hours. But if transcendental style is able to create this movement from abundant to sparse means, it has satisfied at least one universal definition of spiritual art within a "new" medium. It has set a spiritual process in motion.*

Overabundant Means: the Religious Film

If transcendental style represents the proper ratio of abundant to sparse means, it stands to reason that there should then be films overweighted to either side of the ratio, films which use either overly abundant or overly sparse means. The "religious" film, either of the "spectacular" or "inspirational" variety, provides the most common example of the overuse of the abundant artistic means.

Those interested in conveying the Holy on film were among the first to attempt to turn the profane medium to sacred ends. Lumière filmed the Passion Play at Horitz in Bohemia in 1897, Méliès made a fantasy of Christ walking on the waters in 1899, and Zecca created a dramatic film titled *The Prodigal Son* in 1901. Since then film-makers have continually attempted to set the spiritual directly into film. The habitual failure of such "spectacular" and "inspirational" films stems to a large degree from a logical but mistaken notion about the relation between cinematic and spiritual reality. Accepting two assumptions, one, as Ayfre writes, that "the role of cinema . . . is to cause in the spectator . . . the illusion of the Sacred,"[10] and the other, by Durgnat, that "just because the moving photograph satisfies our sense of reality, it is an ideal medium for making fantasy seem

---

* There are many ways one might describe this "spiritual process." I have used Maritain's terms "abundant" and "sparse means" because they have a universal value. Because these terms can be applied universally, however, they lack precision when applied to specific films. Donald Skoller, in an article on Bresson's films, offers a more filmic description of this "spiritual process." He also divides Bresson's films (in this case, *A Man Escaped*) into three stages which reveal a "progressive purification of the visuals." In his terms, the spiritual progression from abundant to sparse means is "a journey through narrative, graphic, and finally plastic levels of being, depicting these phases or zones of the spirit, themselves, through parallel cinematic modalities. He [Fontaine, the protagonist] has gone beyond time and space—the narrative and graphic phases of film—into a realm where things are presented in their essence" ("*Praxis* as a Cinematic Principle in Films by Robert Bresson," *Cinema Journal*, IX, No. 1 [Fall, 1969], pp. 21–22).

real,"[11] the course of action for the religious propagandist was clear: he would simply put the spiritual on film. The film is "real," the spiritual is "on" film, ergo: the spiritual is real. Thus we have an entire history of cinematic magic: the blind are made to see, the lame to walk, the deaf to hear, all on camera.

A classic demonstration of this false syllogism occurs in Cecil B. DeMille's *The Ten Commandments* (1956). In the title scene Moses is on Mount Sinai and God is off-screen to the right. After some premonitory thundering, God literally pitches the commandments, one by one, onto the screen and the awaiting blank tablets. The commandments first appear as small whirling fireballs accompanied by the sound of a rushing wind, and then quickly—building in size all the while—zip across the screen and collide with the blank tablets. Puff! the smoke clears, and the tablet is clearly inscribed. This sort of chicanery apears in a slightly less ridiculous manner in the low budget "inspirational" films.

In the Billy Graham feature, *The Restless Heart*, for example, the cosmic fireball is replaced by a miraculous cure and conversion. In case the viewer may have missed the significance of these acts, a cherubic child appears to inform him that, yes, God still does work miracles. Normally, the spectator does not have "faith" in either of these methods. The slapdash conversion is just as unconvincing as the divine fireball. He knows that the overhand delivery of the commandments was not conceived in heaven, but in some film laboratory, and that the miraculous cure was not due to divine intervention, but to a heavy-handed scriptwriter.

With the exception of some of the more fraudulent DeMille-inspired sex-and-sand epics, many of these films genuinely hope to inspire religious belief. These religious films, like the films of transcendental style, use a decisive action to crystallize their intentions. About seven-eights of the way through the "miracle" occurs, Lazarus plods from his cave, the music soars; why is there no spiritual belief? The truth is, of course, that these films *do* induce a belief; the weeping millions who saw *A Man Called Peter* can testify to that. But this belief cannot honestly be ascribed to the Wholly Other; it is more accurately an affirmative response to a congenial combination of cinematic corporeality and "holy" feelings. And for the many who require no more from sacred art than an emotional experience, these films are sufficient.

The conventional religious film uses a style of identification rather than of confrontation. The style amplifies the abundant artistic means inherent to motion pictures: the viewer is aided and encouraged in his desire to identify and empathize with character, plot, and setting. For an hour or two the viewer can become that suffering, saintly person on screen; his personal problems, guilt and sin are absorbed by humane, noble, and purifying motives. The spiritual drama, like the romantic drama, becomes an escapist metaphor for the human drama. A confrontation between the human and spiritual is avoided. The decisive action is not an unsettling stylistic shock, but the culmination of the abundant means used throughout the film. It fulfills the viewer's fantasy that spirituality can be achieved vicariously; it is the direct result of his identification. The abundant means are indeed tempting to a film-maker, especially if he is bent on proselytizing. With comparative ease he can make an ardent atheist sympathize with the trials and agonies of Christ. But he has not lifted the viewer to Christ's level, he has brought Christ down to the viewer's.

The film-maker intent on expressing the Transcendent must take the other course: he must gradually eliminate the abundant means and the earthly rationale behind them. The moment of confrontation can only occur if, at the decisive action, the abundant means have lost their power. If the "miracle" can be seen in any humanistic tradition, psychological or sociological, the viewer will avoid a confrontation with the Transcendent. By rejecting its own potential over a period of time, cinema can create a style of confrontation. It can set the abundant and sparse means face to face in such a way that the latter seem preferable.

This seemingly self-evident truth about film is something which many aestheticians and theologians, van der Leeuw included, have failed to understand. Van der Leeuw backs up his contention that "rigidity better expresses the deepest nature of things than does movement" by stating, in his only comment on cinema, that "aesthetically and humanly, the puppet theater ranks higher than the cinema."[12] He assumed that films would be restricted to abundant artistic means because they represented real people in actual situations, and that puppets, with their

Overabundant means: Charlton Heston in *The Ten Commandments*. "The conventional religious film uses a style of identification rather than confrontation. It fulfills the viewer's fantasy that spirituality can be achieved vicariously."

sparse stylized faces, would naturally "rank higher." But just the opposite proved to be true: because cinema was so much more "abundant" than puppet theater, it could also be more "sparse," because it was so liberated in technique, it could be more stylized. In cinema's unique ability to reproduce the immanent also lies its unique ability to evoke the Transcendent.

OVERSPARSE MEANS: THE STASIS FILM

A good work can be of "oversparse" means if it fails to sustain life until the process of spiritual purification occurs. The aescetic who starves himself to death out of repentance rather than faith, the church which folds because it won't accept contributions, these would be victims of overly sparse means. "Oversparse" does not mean "oversacred." These means, rather, are not oversparse in principle but in particular: they are too sparse for the particular individual or organization to which they have been applied.

In cinema, therefore, oversparse means would theoretically be those which cannot sustain an audience. Oversparse means in this context should not be mistaken for lack of popularity or small box-office receipts; instead, oversparse means are those which are too sparse too quick. An oversparse film does not allow the viewer to progress from abundant to sparse means. It requires too much of him, demanding instant stasis, and drives him figuratively (and often literally) from the theater.

In *Film Culture* there has been a debate over a type of film which might be called "oversparse." P. Adams Sitney originally described what he called "structural film," and George Maciunas more accurately redefined it as "monomorphic structural film," film "having a single simple form, exhibiting essentially one structural pattern."[13] Within this general category of monomorphic films there is a subcategory I would call stasis films. The films, in terms of transcendental style, are simply extended stasis; they examine a frozen view of life through a duration of time.

The most famous of these "stasis films" is Michael Snow's brilliant *Wavelength*, which is a 45-minute uninterrupted zoom across an apartment loft and "into" a photograph of the sea pinned to the far wall. The over-riding movement of the film is that of the constantly self-restricting camera which examines the still view closer and closer. Bruce Baillie's *Still Life* is a one-shot, fixed-frame, two-minute study of what the title implies, a still life consisting of a tabletop, a floral arrangement, and some table objects. Stan Brakhage's *Song 27, My Mountain* is a 30-minute film study of a Rocky Mountain peak from various angles. Sitney reports that Harry Smith once suggested to Warhol that he film a lengthy fixed shot of Mount Fuji, in which case one would have a concrete case of a transcendental style stasis film—the isolation and prolongation of an Ozu coda.

I don't want to condemn or belittle these films; I would simply like to suggest that, in terms of transcendental style, they employ overly sparse artistic means. Transcendental style builds a spiritual momentum, progressing from abundant to sparse artistic means. To achieve this effect it uses and progressively rejects certain abundant movie devices: character delineation and interaction, linear narrative structure. The stasis films reject even this level of abundant means; they begin at stasis. Transcendental style induces a spiritual movement from everyday to stasis; stasis films require that that movement be already completed. Earlier in this essay I referred to Warhol's static films (*Sleep, Eat, Empire*) as everyday films; they may also be described as stasis films. In Zen terms, both everyday and stasis are the "mountain." Warhol's static films can be thought of as either everyday or stasis films, but, importantly, I do not think they can be thought of as both, effecting movement from one to the other. And movement from abundant to sparse means is our working definition of sacred art.

In order to be effective stasis films require a special knowledge and commitment on the viewer's part. Unless the viewer has a knowledge of past achievements in film and art, and a commitment to explore the spiritual through art, he cannot appreciate the innovation or intention of these films. Stasis films, unlike films of transcendental style, cannot operate on a "cold" unprepared viewer and take him to another level. It is in this sense that the overly sparse stasis films cannot sustain an audience.*

* An important distinction must be made here: these *stasis* films are only oversparse to the extent that they fall into the same category as films of transcendental style. If Warhol's never-filmed Fujiyama film had sought

A Final Definition of Transcendental Style

There is an entire spectrum of abundant artistic means leading to sparse artistic means, just as there is a spectrum of holy feelings leading to a final transcendent attitude. If one did not make this admission he would indeed be on the high road to Beuron. Spirituality in art must have room to move, to change with the times and the arts. The best definition of spiritual art is one that is similarly in flux. It is situated on the spectrum of temporal means and may from time to time move on that spectrum.

In each art and age the transcendental finds its proper level and style. Sometimes that style uses more abundant means, sometimes more sparse means. In film, at present, that level is transcendental style. It represents that point on the spectrum at which the Transcendent is most successfully expressed. If it used more abundant means, it would be less Holy; if it used more sparse means, it would be solipsistic.

Spiritual art must always be in flux because it represents a greater mystery, also in flux, man's relationship to the Holy. In each age the spectator grasps for that special form, that spot on the spectrum, whether in art, religion or philosophy, which can take him to the greater mystery. At present, no film style can perform this crucial task as well as the transcendental style; no films as well as the films of Ozu and Bresson. To expect or settle

---

to evoke the same awareness as *Late Autumn*, then it would have necessarily failed from oversparseness: there simply would have been no attempt to set the spiritual process in motion. But most stasis films, rather than being an extension of transcendental style, are a different breed of film altogether. The best of the stasis films (those by Gehr, Landow, Frampton) attempt, if I understand them, to evoke a transcendental awareness in a method closer to contemporary painting than to the filmic transcendental style. I think, for example, that a fixed-tripod-zoom film like Ernie Gehr's *Serene Velocity* (a 30-minute shot of a corridor quickly intercut from various zoom positions), would be better served rear-projected in an art gallery or home than in a movie theater. Like Kandinsky, these film-makers accept the abundant means as given and operate only within sparse means. This, again, is not to demean the film-painter, but to distinguish him from the film-maker of transcendental style. Of all the stasis film-makers, Michael Snow has come closest to transcendental style in *Wavelength* and he may in fact be evolving a new transcendental style in movies.

for any less from film in general, or the films of Ozu and Bresson in particular, underestimates and demeans them. Transcendental style can take a viewer through the trials of experience to the expression of the Transcendent; it can return him to experience from a calm region untouched by the vagaries of emotion or personality. Transcendental style can bring us nearer to that silence, that invisible image, in which the parallel lines of religion and art meet and interpenetrate.

Notes

Notes to Introduction

1. Carl Jung, *The Secret of the Golden Flower* (New York: Harcourt Brace, 1931), p. 135.

2. Clive Bell, *Art* (London: Chatto & Windus, 1913), p. 68.

3. Gerardus van der Leeuw, *Sacred and Profane Beauty: the Holy in Art* (New York: Holt Rinehart and Winston, 1963), p. 279.

4. Ananda K. Coomaraswamy, "Christian and Oriental Philosophy of Art," *Why Exhibit Works of Art?* (London: Luzac & Co., 1943), p. 53.

5. van der Leeuw, p. 332.

6. Roger Fry, *Vision and Design* (London: Chatto and Windus, 1920), p. 302.

7. Wylie Sypher, *Rococo to Cubism in Art and Literature* (New York: Alfred A. Knopf, 1960), p. xix.

8. Raymond Durgnat, *Films and Feelings* (London: Faber and Faber, Ltd., 1967), p. 30. Arnold Hauser in *The Philosophy of Art History* (New York: Alfred A. Knopf, 1958), p. 120, ascribes the origin of the theory of style as personal expression to Alois Riegl's doctrine of *Kunstwollen*.

9. Heinrich Wolfflin, *Principles of Art History* (New York: Dover Publications, 1950), p. 13.

10. Amédée Ayfre, "Cinéma, et transcendence," *in* Henri Agel and Amédée Ayfre, *Le Cinéma et le sacré* (Paris: Les Editions du Cerf, 1961), p. 157. The late Amédée Ayfre wrote at considerable length about the relationships among transcendence, immanence, incarnation, and the sacred to the cinema. Although this work differs with Ayfre on many points, any study of transcendence and cinema necessarily owes a debt to him.

11. "The Question: Interview with Robert Bresson by Jean-Luc Godard and Michael Delahaye," *Cahiers du Cinéma in English*, No. 8, p. 25.

12. Waldemar Deonna, "Primitivism and Classicism: The Two Faces of Art History," *in* Wylie Sypher (ed.), *Art History: An Anthology of Modern Criticism* (New York: Vintage Books, 1963), p. 26.

13. Ernst Vatter, *Religioese Plastik der Naturvoelkr*, quoted in Robert Goldwater, *Primitivism in Modern Art* (New York: Vintage Books, 1967), p. 39.

Notes to Chapter I

1. St. Ambrose on I Cor. 12:3, cited by St. Thomas Aquinas, *Sum. Theol.*, I–II. 109. I ad I.

2. R. H. Blyth, *Zen in English Literature and Oriental Classics* (New York: E. P. Dutton, 1960), p. 33.

3. D. T. Suzuki, "The Role of Nature in Zen Buddhism," *Zen Buddhism* (Garden City: Doubleday, 1956), pp. 253–256.

4. Donald Richie, *Japanese Movies* (Tokyo: Japan Travel Bureau, 1961), pp. 102–105.

5. Ibid., p. 59.

6. Joseph L. Anderson and Donald Richie, *The Japanese Film* (New York: Grove Press, 1960), p. 51.

7. Tom Milne, "Flavour of Green Tea Over Rice," *Sight and Sound*, 32 (Autumn, 1963), p. 186.

8. Ibid., p. 359.

9. Quoted in Donald Richie, "The Later Films of Yasujiro Ozu," *Film Quarterly*, 13 (Fall, 1959), p. 21.

10. "Ozu on Ozu: The Talkies," *Cinema*, 6 (No. 1), p. 5.

11. Quoted in Richie, "The Later Films . . . ," p. 23.

12. Ibid., p. 22.

13. Richie, "The Later Films . . . ," p. 21.

14. Donald Richie, "Yasujiro Ozu: The Syntax of His Films," *Film Quarterly*, 17 (Winter, 1963–1964).

15. Richie, "The Later Films . . . ," p. 19.

16. J. Blackwell, "Ozu–An Interpretation," paper presented in Film Education course, British Film Institute, London, March, 1968.

17. Ananda K. Coomaraswamy, "Christian and Oriental Philosophy of Art," *Why Exhibit Works of Art?* (London: Luzac, 1943), p. 41.

18. Richie, "Yasujiro Ozu: The Syntax . . . ," p. 13.

19. Richie, *Japanese Movies*, p. 75.

20. Letter from Donald Richie, Department of Film, Museum of Modern Art, New York, N.Y., March 9, 1970.

21. Letter from Donald Richie, April 6, 1970.

22. William K. Barnes (ed.), *Religions in Japan*, a report prepared by the Religious and Cultural Resources Division, Civil Information and Education Section, General Headquarters of the Supreme Commander of the Allied Powers, Tokyo (Tokyo: Charles E. Tuttle Company, Inc., 1955), p. 90.

23. Alan W. Watts, *The Spirit of Zen* (New York: Grove Press, 1960), p. 43.

24. Langdon Warner, *The Enduring Art of Japan* (New York: Grove Press, 1958), p. 99.

25. Milne, p. 184.

26. Will Peterson, "Stone Garden," *in* Nancy Wilson Ross (ed.), *The World of Zen* (New York: Vintage Books, 1960), p. 107.

27. Richie, "Yasujiro Ozu: The Syntax . . . . ," p. 12.

28. Peterson, p. 109.

29. Alan W. Watts, *The Way of Zen* (New York: Pantheon, 1957), p. 183.

30. Richie, "Yasujiro Ozu: The Syntax ...," p. 15.

31. Ananda K. Coomaraswamy, "The Theory of Art in Asia," *The Transformation of Nature in Art* (New York: Dover Publications, 1956), pp. 30–31.

32. Watts, *The Way of Zen*, p. 176.

33. Richie, "The Later Films ...," p. 24.

34. Richie, "A Short Guide to the Aesthetics of Japanese Film," *Unijapan Bulletin*, 2 (December, 1965), p. 2.

35. Suzuki, p. 231.

36. Ibid., p. 240.

37. Watts, *The Way of Zen*, p. 187.

38. "A Talk with Ozu," *Cinema*, 6 (No. 1), p. 7.

39. "Ozu on Ozu ...," p. 4.

40. Anderson and Richie, p. 359.

41. Amédée Ayfre, "Cinéma et transcendence," *in* Henri Agel and Amédée Ayfre, *Le Cinéma et le sacré* (Paris: Les Editions du Cerf, 1961), p. 154.

42. Jean Sémolué, "Les Personnages de Robert Bresson," *Cashiers du Cinéma*, 13 (October, 1957), p. 12.

43. Ayfre, p. 165.

44. Tadao Sato, *The Art of Yasujiro Ozu* (Tokyo: Japan Independent Film, 1966), p. 13.

45. Richie has pointed out that "humor in Japan is often malicious, even usually. Ozu is using common humor here. Irony is rare—many Japanese never understood that Ozu is ironical" (Letter, April 6, 1970). Even if the Japanese did not understand Ozu's ironic humor, it is safe to say that through disparity Ozu operated within the ironic mode, as do Bresson and Dreyer.

46. Milne, p. 183.

47. Suzuki, p. 234.

48. Sato, p. 22.

49. Christopher Dawson, *Religion and Culture* (Cleveland: World Publishing, 1958), pp. 36–37.

50. Ruldolf Otto, *Mysticism East and West* (New York: Collier Books, 1962), p. 57 f.

51. Warner, p. 103. Warner's quote points out an interesting semantic difficulty about the term transcendence. Etymologically transcendence means *trans*, across, and *scandare*, to climb; implying, of course, that it has more affinity with conversion than *satori*. My use, however, is not bound by etymological restrictions and refers to the common spiritual experience shared by all cultures.

52. D. T. Suzuki, *Mysticism Christian and Buddhist* (New York: Collier Books, 1962), p. 101.

Notes to Chapter II

1. Raymond Durgnat, "*Les Anges du Péché*," *in* Jan Cameron (ed.), *The Films of Robert Bresson* (London: Studio Vista, 1969), p. 25.

2. Susan Sontag, "Spiritual Style in the Films of Robert Bresson," *Against Interpretation* (New York: Farrar Straus & Giroux, 1966), p. 186.

3. "Interview recueilli par Michel Capdenac," *Les Lettres Françaises*, No. 928 (May 24, 1962).

4. Raymond Durgnat, *Films and Feelings* (London: Faber and Faber, 1967), p. 41.

5. James Blue, *Excerpts from an Interview with Robert Bresson June, 1965* (Los Angeles: by the author, 1969), p. 2.

6. Sontag, p. 180.

7. Quoted in Marjorie Greene, "Robert Bresson," *Film Quarterly*, 13 (Spring, 1960), p. 6.

8. "The Question: Interview with Robert Bresson by Jean-Luc Godard and Michael Delahaye," *Cashiers du Cinéma in English*, No. 8, p. 12.

9. Gervase Mathew, *Byzantine Aesthetics* (London: John Murray, 1963), p. 6.

10. "Excerpts . . . ," p. 1.

11. "Propos de Robert Bresson," *Cashiers du Cinéma*, 13 (October, 1957), p. 4.

12. "Excerpts . . . ," p. 2.

13. Amédée Ayfre, "The Universe of Robert Bresson," *in* Cameron (ed.), *The Films of Robert Bresson*, p. 8.

14. Interview with Jean Pelegri, actor in *Pickpocket*, by James Blue, January, 1961.

15. "Interview," *L'Express*, December 23, 1959.

16. "The Question," p. 25.

17. Sontag, p. 191.

18. Quoted in Roy Armes, *French Cinema Since 1946*, Vol. I: *The Great Tradition* (Cranbury, N.J.: A. S. Barnes, 1966), p. 120.

19. Quoted in Jean Douchet, "Bresson on Location," *Sequence*, No. 13 (New Year, 1951), p. 8.

20. "Excerpts . . . ," p. 2.

21. Quoted in Sontag, p. 185.

22. Quoted in Armes, p. 121.

23. "The Question," p. 16.

24. "Interview recueilli par Michel Capdenac."

25. André Bazin, "*Le Journal d'un Curé de Campagne* and the Stylistics of Robert Bresson," *What is Cinema?* (Berkeley: University of California Press, 1967), p. 133.

26. "The Question," p. 16.

27. "Excerpts . . . ," p. 2.

28. Quoted in Roland Monod, "Working with Bresson," *Sight and Sound*, 26 (Summer, 1957), p. 31.

29. "Excerpts . . . ," p. 4.

30. "Interview recueilli par Michel Capdenac."

31. "Excerpts . . . ," p. 1.

32. Bazin, p. 128.

33. Quoted in John Russell Taylor, *Cinema Eye, Cinema Ear* (New York: Hill and Wang, 1964), p. 130.

34. Sontag, pp. 183–184.

35. "Excerpts . . . ," pp. 3–4.

36. Sontag, p. 179.

37. Ibid., p. 183.

38. Jean Sémolué, *Bresson* (Paris: Editions Universitaires, 1959), p. 69.

39. "Entretien avec Robert Bresson et Jean Guitton," *Etudes Cinématographiques*, Nos. 18–19 (Autumn, 1962), pp. 93–94.

40. "Excerpts . . . ," p. 2.

41. Jean Sémolué, "Les Personages de Robert Bresson," *Cahiers du Cinéma*, 13 (October, 1957), p. 12.

42. "Excerpts . . . ," p. 4.

43. "Interview," *Arts*, June 17, 1959.

44. Quoted in Armes, p. 123.

45. "Excerpts . . . ," p. 4.

46. Quoted in Leo Murray, "*Un Condamné à Mort S'est Echappé*," in Cameron (ed.), *The Films of Robert Bresson*, p. 79.

47. "Propos de Robert Bresson," p. 7.

48. "Excerpts . . . ," p. 4.

49. John Dewey, *Art As Experience* (New York: Capricorn Books, 1958), p. 69.

50. Ayfre, "The Universe . . . ," pp. 14–15.

51. Quoted in Murray, p. 68.

52. Sontag, p. 189.

53. "Propos de Robert Bresson," p. 6.

54. Quoted in Heinz Skrobucha, *Icons* (London: Oliver & Boyd, 1963), p. 21.

55. Quoted in Jacques Maritain, *Art and Scholasticism and the Frontiers of Poetry* (New York: Charles Scribner's Sons, 1962), p. 67.

56. Ibid.

57. Plato, *Phaedo* 67 D.

58. Calvin, *Inst.* I, XV, 2.

59. Quoted in Marvin Zeman, "The Suicide of Robert Bresson," *Cinema* VI, No. 3 (Spring, 1971), p. 37.

60. Ibid.

61. Quoted in Greene, p. 9.

62. "The Question," p. 10.

63. Bazin, p. 134.

64. Jansen, *Augustinus* XI, p. 131.

65. "The Question," p. 25.

66. Quoted in Ayfre, "The Universe . . . ," p. 24.

67. Ananda K. Coomaraswamy, "The Theory of Art in Asia," *The Transformation of Nature in Art* (Cambridge: Harvard University Press, 1934), p. 3.

68. Maritain, p. 10.

69. Coomaraswamy, p. 57.

70. Aquinas, *In Poster. Analyst.* lib. I, Lect. 1, No. 1.

71. Erwin Panofsky, *Gothic Architecture and Scholasticism* (New York: Meridian Books, 1958), pp. 28–29.

72. Ibid., p. 64.

73. Quoted in Manolis Chatzidakis and André Grabar, *Byzantine and Early Medieval Painting* (New York: Viking Press, 1965), pp. 4–5.

74. A. C. Bridge; *Images of God* (London: Hodder and Stroughton, 1960), p. 33.

75. Ibid., p. 51.

76. Barthélémy Amengual, "Rapports avec l'art byzantine," *S. M. Eisenstein,* Premier Plan No. 25 (October, 1962), p. 97.

77. Quoted in Skrobucha, p. 9.

78. Agathias, *Palatine Anthology,* quoted in Mathew, p. 78.

79. Gerardus van der Leeuw, *Sacred and Profane Beauty: the Holy in Art* (New York: Holt Rinehart and Winston, 1963), p. 304.

80. Quoted in Herbert Read, *Art and Society* (New York: Schocken Books, 1966), p. 58.

81. Quoted in Skrobucha, p. 6.

Notes to Chapter III

1. "Between Heaven and Hell: Interview with Carl Dreyer by Michel Delahaye," *Cahiers du Cinema in English,* No. 4, p. 12.

2. Claude Perrin, *Carl. Th. Dreyer* (Paris: Editions Seghers, 1969), p. 87.

3. Lotte H. Eisner, *The Haunted Screen* (Berkeley: University of California Press, 1969), pp. 177–221.

4. Ibid., p. 177.

5. August Strindberg. *Open Letters to the Intimate Theater,* trans. and ed. by Walter Johnson (Seattle: University of Washington Press, 1959), p. 19.

6. Eisner, p. 179.

7. Lotte H. Eisner, "Recontre avec Carl Dreyer," *Cahiers du Cinéma,* 9 (June, 1955), p. 5.

8. "Between Heaven and Hell . . . ," p. 15.

9. Carl Dreyer, "A Little on Film Style," *Cinema,* 6 (Fall, 1970), p. 10.

10. Ibid., p. 11.

11. Carl Dreyer, "Thoughts on My Craft," *Sight and Sound,* 25 (Winter, 1955–56), p. 129.

12. "Interview with Dreyer by John H. Winge," *Sight and Sound,* 19 (January, 1950), p. 17.

13. "Filmographie Commentée," *Cahiers du Cinéma,* No. 207 (December, 1968), p. 72.

14. Dreyer, "A Little . . . ," p. 10.

15. Ibid.

16. "Between Heaven and Hell . . . ," p. 8.

17. "Propos de Robert Bresson," Cashiers du Cinéma, 13 (October, 1957), p. 4.

18. Jean Sémolué, "Passion et Procès (de Dreyer à Bresson)," Études Cinématographiques, Nos. 18–19 (Autumn, 1962), p. 106.

19. Richard Rowland writes that The Passion of Joan of Arc is the "splendid solitude of a pure and determined woman" (Cine-Technician, [January–February, 1951], p. 5).

20. Boerge Trolle writes, "Is the Swedish critic Gerd Osten right when, in interpreting Dreyer's work in psychological terms, she puts forward the suggestion that the fear of women plays a much more important part than has been previously suggested?" ("The World of Carl Dreyer," Sight and Sound, 25 [Winter, 1955–56], p. 126).

21. Robert Warshow, "Day of Wrath: The Enclosed Image," The Immediate Experience (Garden City: Anchor Books, 1964), p. 196 f.

22. Dreyer, "A Little . . . ," p. 10.

23. Trolle, p. 126.

24. Perrin, p. 101.

25. Wilhelm Worringer, Abstraction and Empathy (Cleveland: World Publishing Company, 1967), p. 134.

26. Wilhelm Worringer, Form in Gothic (New York: Schocken Books, 1964), p. 81.

27. Arnold Hauser, The Social History of Art, Vol. I: Prehistoric, Ancient-Oriental, Greece and Rome, Middle Ages (New York: Vintage Books, 1951), pp. 234–235.

28. Wylie Sypher, Four Stages of Renaissance Style (Garden City: Anchor Books, 1955), p. 46.

29. Worringer, Form in Gothic, p. 68.

30. Emile Male, Religious Art from the Twelfth to the Eighteenth Century (New York: Noonday Press, 1958), p. 199.

31. Worringer, Form in Gothic, p. 81.

32. Sypher, p. 54.

33. André Grabar, The Art of the Byzantine Empire (New York: Crown Publishers, 1966), p. 108.

34. Paul Tillich, Theology of Culture (New York: Oxford University Press, 1964), p. 75.

35. Henri Daniel-Rops, The Church in the Dark Ages Vol II (Garden City: Image Books, 1962), p. 271.

Notes to Conclusion

1. Jacques Maritain, Art and Scholasticism and the Frontiers of Poetry (New York: Charles Scribner's Sons, 1962), p. 103.

2. Wassily Kandinsky, Concerning the Spiritual in Art (New York: George Wittenborn, 1964), p. 66.

3. Jacques Maritain, "Religion and Culture," The Social and Political Philosophy of Jacques Maritain (Garden City: Image Books, 1965), p. 219.

4. Gerardus van der Leeuw, *Sacred and Profane Beauty* (New York: Holt, Rinehart and Winston, 1963), p. 172.

5. André Bazin, "The Ontology of the Photographic Image," *What Is Cinema?* (Berkeley: University of California Press, 1967), p. 11.

6. Wyler Sypher, *Rococo to Cubism in Art and Literature* (New York: Vintage Books, 1960), p. 73.

7. Ibid., pp. 265–267.

8. Bazin, "The Ontology . . . ," p. 12.

9. The effect of cinema on the "psychological" literature of Joyce and Proust, for example, is discussed in Arnold Hauser, *The Social History of Art* Vol. IV: *Naturalism, Impressionism, The Film Age* (New York: Vintage Books, 1951), pp. 238–239.

10. Amédée Ayfre, "Cinéma et transcendence," *Le Cinéma et le sacré,* Henri Agel and Amédée Ayfre (Paris: Les Editions du Cerf, 1961), p. 159.

11. Raymond Durgnat, *Films and Feelings* (London: Faber and Faber, 1967), p. 31.

12. van der Leeuw, 162.

13. George Macuinas, "Some Comments on *Structural Film* by P. Adams Sitney," *Film Culture Reader* (New York: Praeger Publishers, 1970), p. 349.

Selected Bibliography

The following bibliography is personal; these books and essays, to varying degrees, directly influenced the writing of this essay. Whenever possible, original English editions are listed.

Aesthetics

Agel, Henri, and Amédée Ayfre. *Le Cinéma et le sacré*. Paris: Les Editions du Cerf, 1961.
Arnheim, Rudolf. *Art and Visual Perception*. Berkeley: University of California Press, 1954.
Ayfre, Amédée. *Le Cinéma et la foi chrétienne*. Paris: Librairie Arthème Fayard, 1960.
———. *Cinéma et mystère*. Paris: Les Editions du Cerf, 1969.
———. *Conversion aux images?* Paris: Les Editions du Cerf, 1964.
———. *Dieu au cinéma*. Paris: Ed. Privat, Presses Universitaires de France, 1953.
Bazin, André. *What is Cinema?* Berkeley: University of California Press, 1967.
Bell, Clive. *Art*. London: Chatto & Windus, 1913.
Bridge, A. C. *Images of God*. London: Hodder and Stroughton, 1960.
Collingwood, R. G. *The Principles of Art*. Oxford: Clarendon Press, 1938.
Coomaraswamy, Ananda K. *The Transformation of Nature in Art*. Cambridge: Harvard University Press, 1934.
———. *Why Exhibit Works of Art?* London: Luzac, 1943.
Cope, Gilbert, ed. *Christianity and the Visual Arts*. London: The Faith Press, 1964.
Dawson, Christopher. *Religion and Culture*. New York: Sheed and Ward, 1948.
Dewey, John. *Art As Experience*. New York: G. P. Putnam's Sons, 1934.
Durgnat, Raymond. *Films and Feelings*. Cambridge: The M.I.T. Press, 1967.
Eliade, Mircea. *Patterns in Comparative Religion*. New York: Sheed and Ward, 1958.
———. *The Sacred and the Profane*. New York: Harcourt, Brace & World, 1959.
Fry, Roger. *Vision and Design*. London: Chatto & Windus, 1925.
Goldwater, Robert. *Primitivism in Modern Art*. New York: Harper, 1938.
Hauser, Arnold. *The Philosophy of Art History*. New York: Alfred A. Knopf, 1958.
———. *The Social History of Art*. New York: Alfred A. Knopf, 1951.
Huxley, Aldous. *On Art and Artists*. Cleveland: World Publishing, 1960.
Isherwood, Christopher. "The Problem of the Religious Novel,"

———. *Exhumations.* Harmondsworth, England: Penguin Books Ltd., 1966.

Jarrett-Kerr, Martin. "Theology and the Arts," *The Scope of Theology.* Edited by Daniel T. Jenkins. Cleveland: World Publishing, 1968.

Jung, Carl G. *Psychology and Religion.* London: Oxford University Press, 1938.

Kandinsky, Wassily. *Concerning the Spiritual in Art.* New York: George Wittenborn, 1947.

Langer, Susanne K. *Feeling and Form.* New York: Charles Scribner's Sons, 1953.

———. *Problems in Art.* New York: Charles Scribner's Sons, 1957.

Male, Emile, *Religious Art in France of the Thirteenth Century.* New York: E. P. Dutton, 1913.

———. *Religious Art from the Twelfth to the Eighteenth Century.* New York: Pantheon, 1949.

Maritain, Jacques. *Art and Scholasticism and the Frontiers of Poetry.* New York: Charles Scribner's Sons, 1962.

———. "Religion and Culture," *The Social and Political Philosophy of Jacques Maritain.* Garden City: Doubleday, 1965.

Mathew, Gervase. *Byzantine Aesthetics.* London: John Murray, 1963.

Morey, Charles Rufus. *Christian Art.* New York: Longmans, 1935.

Niebuhr, H. Richard. *Christ and Culture.* New York: Harper and Row, 1951.

Otto, Rudolph. *Mysticism East and West.* New York: Macmillan, 1932.

Panofsky, Erwin. *Gothic Architecture and Scholasticism.* New York: Meridian, 1958.

———. *Meaning in the Visual Arts.* Garden City: Doubleday, 1955.

———. *Studies in Iconology.* New York: Oxford University Press, 1939.

Read, Herbert. *Art and Society.* London: Faber & Faber, 1945.

———. *The Meaning of Art.* London: Faber & Faber, 1931.

Rowland, Benjamin, Jr. *Art in East and West.* Cambridge: Harvard University Press, 1954.

Sitney, P. Adams. "Structural Film," *Film Culture,* No. 47 (Summer, 1969).

Suzuki, Daisetz Teitaro. *Mysticism Christian and Buddhist.* New York: Collier Books, 1962.

Sypher, Wylie. *Rococo to Cubism.* Alfred A. Knopf, 1960.

Tillich, Paul. *The Religious Situation.* New York: Meridian, 1956.

———. *Theology of Culture.* New York: Oxford University Press, 1964.

van der Leeuw, Gerardus. *Sacred and Profane Beauty: the Holy in Art.* New York: Holt, Rinehart and Winston, 1963.

Von Ogden Vogt. *Art and Religion.* New Haven: Yale University Press, 1921.

Wolfflin, Heinrich. *Classic Art.* London: Phaidon, 1952.

———. *Principles of Art History.* New York: Dover Publications, 1950.

Worringer, Wilhelm. *Abstraction and Empathy.* London: Routledge and Kegan Paul, 1948.

———. *Form in Gothic.* New York: G. P. Putnam's Sons, 1927.

CHAPTER I: OZU

Anderson, Joseph L., and Donald Richie. *The Japanese Film.* Tokyo: Charles E. Tuttle, 1959.

Binyon, Lawrence. *The Spirit of Man in Asian Art.* Cambridge: Harvard University Press, 1935.

Blyth, R. H. *Zen in English Literature and Oriental Classics.* Tokyo:

Hokuseido Press, 1948.
Giularis, Shinobu and Marcel. *Le Cinéma Japanais*. Paris: Les Editions du Cerf, 1956.
Herrigel, E. *Zen in the Art of Archery*. New York: Pantheon, 1953.
Milne, Tom. "Flavour of Green Tea Over Rice," *Sight and Sound*, 32 (Autumn, 1963).
"Ozu Spectrum," *Cinema* (Beverly Hills), 6, No. 1.
Richie, Donald. "Bibliography," *Film Comment*, 7 (Spring, 1971).
————. *Japanese Movies*. Tokyo: Japan Travel Bureau, 1961.
————. "The Later Films of Yasujiro Ozu," *Film Quarterly*, 13 (Fall, 1959).
————. "A Short Guide to the Aesthetics of Japanese Film," *UniJapan Bulletin*, Nos. 11–12 (December, 1965).
————. "Yasujiro Ozu: The Syntax of His Films," *Film Quarterly*, 17 (Winter, 1963–1964).
Ryu, Chishu. "Yasujiro Ozu," *Sight and Sound*, 33 (Spring, 1964).
Sato, Tadao. *The Art of Yasujiro Ozu*. Tokyo: Japan Independent Film, 1966.
Siren, O. "Zen Buddhism and its Relation to Art," *Theosophical Path*. Point Loma, Calif., 1934.
Suzuki, Daisetz Teitaro. *Essays in Zen Buddhism*. 3 vols. London: Luzac, 1927, 1933, 1934.
————. *Zen Buddhism and Its Influence on Japanese Culture*. Kyoto: Eastern Buddhist Society, 1938.
Warner, Langdon. *The Enduring Art of Japan*. Cambridge: Harvard University Press, 1952.
Watts, Alan W. *The Spirit of Zen*. London: Murray, 1936.
————. *The Way of Zen*. New York: Pantheon, 1957.
Wood, Robin. "Tokyo Story," *Movie*, No. 13 (Summer, 1965)

CHAPTER II: BRESSON

Armes, Roy. *French Cinema Since 1946*. Vol. I, *The Great Tradition*. London: Zwemmer, 1966.
Blue, James. *Excepts from an Interview with Robert Bresson, June 1965*. Los Angeles: by the author, 1969.
Briot, René. *Robert Bresson*. Paris: Les Editions du Cerf, 1957.
Cameron, Ian, ed. *The Films of Robert Bresson*. London: Studio Vista, 1969.
Chatzidakis, Manolis, and André Grabar. *Byzantine and Early Medieval Painting*. London: George Weidenfeld and Nicholson, 1965.
Douchet, Jean. "Bresson on Location," *Sequence*, No. 13 (New Year, 1951).
Drouguet, Robert. *Robert Bresson*. Lyon: Premier Plan 42, SERDOC, 1966.
"Entretien avec Robert Bresson," *Cahiers du Cinéma*, No. 104 (February, 1960).
"Entretien avec Robert Bresson," *Cahiers du Cinéma*, No. 140 (February, 1963).
Estève, Michel. *Robert Bresson*. Paris: Seghers, 1962.
Grabar, André. *The Art of the Byzantine Empire*. London: Methuen, 1966.
Green, Calvin. "Ars Theologica," *Cineaste*, 3 (Fall, 1969).
Green, Julien. "En Travaillant avec Robert Bresson," *Cahiers du Cinéma*, No. 50 (August–September, 1955).
Green, Marjorie. "Robert Bresson," *Film Quarterly*, 13 (Spring, 1960).
Hussey, J. M. *The Byzantine World*. London: Hutchinson, 1957.
"Interview with Robert Bresson," *Movie*, No. 7 (February–March, 1963).

Lambert, Gavin. "Notes on Robert Bresson," *Sight and Sound*, 23 (July–September, 1953).
Lethaby, W. R. *Mediaeval Art*. London: Duckworth, 1904.
Mayersburg, Paul. "The Trial of Joan of Arc," *Movie*, No. 7 (February–March, 1963).
Monod, Roland. "Working with Bresson," *Sight and Sound*, 27 (Summer, 1957).
Morey, Charles Rufus. *Mediaeval Art*. New York: Norton, 1942.
"Propos de Robert Bresson," *Cahiers du Cinéma*, No. 75 (October, 1957).
"The Question: Interview with Robert Bresson," *Cahiers du Cinema in English*, No. 8.
Rhode, Eric. *Tower of Babel*. London: Weidenfeld & Nicholson, 1966.
Rice, David Talbot. *Byzantine Art*. London: Oxford University Press, 1935.
Roud, Richard. "The Early Work of Robert Bresson," *Film Culture*, No. 20 (1959).
Sémolué, Jean. *Bresson*. Paris: Editions Universitaires, 1959.
Skrobucha, Heinz. *Icons*. London: Oliver & Boyd, 1963.
Sontag, Susan. *Against Interpretation*. New York: Farrar, Strauss & Giroux, 1966.
Taylor, John Russell. *Cinema Eye, Cinema Ear*. London: Methuen, 1964.
Wulf, Maurice de. *History of Medieval Philosophy*, 2 vols. London: Longmas, Green, 1938.
Zeman, Marvin. "The Suicide of Robert Bresson," *Cinema* (Beverly Hills), 6 (Spring, 1971).

CHAPTER III: DREYER

Adams, Henry. *Mont-Saint-Michel and Chartres*. New York: American Institute of Architects, 1913.
Agee, James. "Day of Wrath," *Agee on Film*. Boston: Beacon Press, 1964.
Amengual, Barthélémy. "Bresson et Dreyer," *Image et Son*, No. 69 (February, 1954).
"Between Heaven and Hell, Interview with Carl Dreyer," *Cahiers du Cinema in English*, No. 4.
Bond, Kirk. "The Basic Demand of Life for Love," *Film Comment*, 4 (Fall, 1966).
————. "The World of Carl Dreyer," *Film Quarterly*, 19 (Fall, 1965).
Bowser, Eileen. "The Films of Carl Dreyer." New York: The Museum of Modern Art, 1964.
"Carl Dreyer," *Cahiers du Cinéma*, special issue, No. 207 (December, 1968).
Cowie, Peter. "Dreyer at 75," *Films and Filming* (March, 1964).
Daniel-Rops, Henri. *The Church in the Dark Ages*, 2 vols. New York: E. P. Dutton & Co., 1960.
Dreyer, Carl. "Color and Color Films," *Films in Review* (April, 1955).
————. "Ecrits de Carl Dreyer, I–IV," *Cahiers du Cinéma*, Nos. 124, 127, 133, 134.
————. "A Little on Film Style," *Cinema* (Beverly Hills), 6 (Fall, 1970).
————. "Metaphysic of *Ordet*: A Letter from Carl Th. Dreyer," *Film Culture*, No. 7.
————. "Thoughts on my Craft," *Sight and Sound*, 25 (Winter, 1955–56).
Duperly, Denis. "Carl Dreyer: Utter Bore or Total Genius?", *Films and Filming* (February, 1968).

Eisner, Lotte H. "Réalisme et Irréel Chez Dreyer," *Cahiers du Cinéma*, No. 65.

──────. "Recontre avec Carl Dreyer," *Cahiers du Cinéma*, 9, No. 48.

Esteve, Michel, ed. *Jeanne d' Arc à l'écran. Etudes Cinématographiques*, Nos. 18–19 (Autumn, 1962).

──────. *La Passion du Christ, Etudes Cinématographiques*, Nos. 10–11 (Autumn, 1961).

"Interview with Dreyer," *Sight and Sound*, 19 (January, 1950).

Kelman, Ken. "Dreyer," *Film Culture*, No. 35 (Winter, 1964–65).

Manvell, Roger. "Lunch with Carl Dreyer," *Pequin Film Review*, No. 3 (1947).

Martindale, Andrew. *Gothic Art*. New York: Praeger, 1967.

Monty, I. B., "Carl Th. Dreyer," Copenhagen: Danish Governmental Film Foundation, 1964.

"My Way of Working is in Relation to the Future, A Conversation with Carl Dreyer," *Film Comment*, 4 (Fall, 1966).

Neergaard, Ebbe. *Carl Dreyer: A Film Director's Work*. London: British Film Institute, 1955.

Parrain, Phillippe, Barthélémy Amengual, and Vincent Pinel. *Dreyer: Cadres et Mouvements. Etudes Cinématographiques*, Nos. 53–56 (1967).

Perrin, Claude. *Carl Th. Dreyer*. Paris: Editions Seghers, 1969.

Powell, Dilys. "Carl Dreyer," *Film Today* (1948).

Rohmer, Eric. "Une Alceste chrétienne: *Ordet*," *Cahiers du Cinéma*, No. 55.

Rowland, Richard. "Carl Dreyer's World," *The Cine-Technician* (January-February, 1951).

Sémolué, Jean. *Dreyer*. Paris: Editions Universitaires, 1962.

──────. "Quelques Réflexions sur Dreyer et sur Bresson," *Education et Cinéma*, Nos. 15–16 (October–November, 1958).

Scott, Geoffrey. *The Architecture of Humanism*. London: Constable and Co., 1924.

Skoller, Don. "A Little on Film Style: Annotations," *Cinema* (Beverly Hills), 6 (Fall, 1970).

──────. "To Rescue *Gertrud*," *Film Comment*, 4 (Fall, 1966).

Sypher, Wylie. *Four Stages of Renaissance Style*. Garden City: Doubleday, 1955.

Trolle, Boerge. "The World of Carl Dreyer," *Sight and Sound*, 25 (Winter, 1955–56).

Warshow, Robert. "*Day of Wrath*: The Enclosed Image," *The Immediate Experience*. Garden City: Doubleday, 1962.

Index

Index